GOOD NIGHT, GOD BLESS

A family bedtime book

Michael Forster

ILLUSTRATED BY
JENNIFER CARTER

Kevin Mayhew

First published in 1995 by
KEVIN MAYHEW LTD
Rattlesden
Bury St Edmunds
Suffolk IP30 0SZ

ISBN 0 86209 701 0
Catalogue No 1500031

Cover illustration by Jennifer Carter

Edited by Peter Dainty and Alison Sommazzi
Typesetting and Page Creation by Vicky Brown
Printed and bound in Great Britain.

FOREWORD

Getting children to bed can be an activity which takes us through the whole gamut of emotions from exasperation to hilarity. The intention of this book, which follows the pattern of *A Story, a Hug and a Prayer*, is that it should be fun while also being a chance to explore ideas. Most important, though, is that it should be an opportunity to enjoy and develop the relationships within which we all grow and in which we encounter God.

The traditional practice of kneeling at the side of the bed would not be the best way to use this book; it's really about relating – to each other first, and thereby to God. So use it as freely as you like, with plenty of ad libs, laughs and cuddles, and don't be afraid to be undignified! It is my profound belief, and earnest hope, that God has a sense of humour and loves to be involved in the fun we have. So although the stories and the prayers will certainly include some serious moments, it is important that they should not become heavy. Most of all, they must be a positive experience of love and the assurance of God's care. In particular, the confession which is part of every set of prayers should be a chance for unburdening and reassurance, not the building up of more guilt and this is a point where a cuddle might be especially appropriate.

Please take these stories and prayers and make them your own; but most importantly of all, *enjoy* them. Then I firmly believe that God will, as well.

MICHAEL FORSTER

Contents

LET IT BE

Before God made the world, everything was very, very dark. The universe was shapeless and had no life in it, except for God. In the silence, the only sound was of God breathing. Then God spoke.

'Let there be light!'

And suddenly, there was light everywhere. Just imagine having all the lights in your street burning in your bedroom. It was brilliant! The trouble was, there was no one there to see it, except God. But he was working on that.

God looked at the light, and said, 'That's pretty good, but it wouldn't do to have it always. I know. I'll create time.' So he divided up light from darkness. 'There,' he said. 'That's the day, and I'll call *that* the night.' So the evening came, and then the morning, and that was the very first day. But things were still in a pretty disordered state – a bit like most children's bedrooms, only a million times worse! So God decided it was time to do some sorting out. 'There,' he said, when he had finished. 'I'll call this part "heaven".' By that time it was evening, and after that came another morning: the second day.

Well, there was an awful lot of water sloshing about in the world, and God decided that was the next bit to be tidied up. 'Let's get all the water together,' he said, 'and make a bit of dry land. I'll call the dry bits "earth" and the watery bits "sea". My Word, that looks good!' Then God really started to get going! 'Now, let's see what this earth can produce!' he said. 'Give me some plants!' And it happened. 'Give me some seeds,' said God. And it happened. 'Give me some fruit!' And before long, the earth was covered with wonderful green plants, and brightly coloured fruit: red strawberries, yellow bananas – what else can you think of? 'Well, bless me!' thought God. 'This is really good!' But by now – yes, you've guessed it – the evening had come again. Then came the morning, and that was the third day.

The earth was looking pretty spectacular. So God looked around at the sky and thought, 'I'd better spruce this up a bit.

Let's have some stars, and planets around here. And they'd better move round in circles to mark the seasons of the year – or else we'll end up with May blossom in November or something equally silly.' So God provided a bright light for the day, and a dimmer one at night – just enough to stop it being too frightening. By then it was evening again, and God said, 'Well upon my Word – that's a good day's work!' Then he waited for morning. The fourth day had gone.

Now there were all kinds of plants and flowers on the earth, wonderful stars in the sky, but the sea was looking a bit empty. So God spoke to the sea. 'Let's see what you can do,' he said. 'Give me lots of animals – great big sea monsters, and whales and sharks, and octopuses. And let's have some birds in the air as well.' Before you could say – well, you couldn't say anything because people hadn't happened yet – but anyway, there were fish and birds all over the place. Then God said, 'That's right – make yourselves at home, and let's have lots of you – I want plenty of life in the world!' And then what do you think? That's right – it was evening again. That was the fifth day.

When morning came, God looked at the earth, and said, 'Come on – let's have some life around here! Don't leave it all to the sea.' So that's exactly what happened. Every kind of wild animal – everything from dinosaurs to dingoes! And God was pleased – but not *that* pleased! 'What would really top it off,' he said, 'would be people; human beings, made like me, able to love and be loved, who would be my special friends. They'd be able to help me – we could do things together. They would be the best of all the things I've made.' So God made men and women; he made them able to love, and able to think, and said, 'Come and be my special friends and helpers. Share my work of making this creation a wonderful place to be. Look, I've given you great things – plants and fruit and rocks, wonderful colours, and everything you could ever need. Look after it well, and work with me to make it even better.'

And so it was. God looked at everything he had made, and thought, 'Even though I say it myself, it's pretty terrific!' That was the sixth day.

Then the morning came again: the seventh day. And what do you think God did then? He had a rest!

Based on Genesis 1

Let's Chat

What do you most like about the world?
Beautiful countryside? Flowers? People?
What else?

We're Sad

We're sorry, God,
for all the things that spoil your world.
Sometimes we forget just how beautiful
and how fragile it is.
Forgive us, and help us
to care for your creation.

We're Glad

The world's a wonderful place:
full of colour, and light and life.
Thank you for making it beautiful in so many ways.
And thank you especially
for letting us help you.

Let's Pray for People

There are some people who can't see or hear
the beautiful things in the world.
And some just don't notice,
because they're too busy.
Please, God, help all people
to enjoy your creation
in lots of different ways.

Snake in the Grass

Cecil the serpent was hiding in some bushes, thinking what a lot of fun he was going to have getting his own back. When God had made the garden, Cecil had thought he was going to be put in charge of it. Then imagine his horror when God created a completely new kind of animal and put *them* in charge. Human beings, they were called. Well, that was a silly name for an animal to begin with, and they were such newcomers! Actually, Cecil hadn't been there all that long either, as it was a new garden, but because he had been there just that bit longer he thought that made him better. 'These new animals!' he thought. 'They come in here and think they own the place!' Then he overheard God talking to the humans.

'Now,' said God, 'you can eat any fruit you find in the garden, except the fruit on that tree in the middle.'

'Why?' asked the female human, who was called Eve.

'It's the tree of knowledge,' said God, 'the knowledge of right and wrong, and you must not eat from it or you will die.'

Cecil waited a few minutes and squirmed up close to Eve.

'Ooh!' yelled Eve. 'You didn't half frighten me. What do you think you're doing, sneaking up on people like that?'

'Oh,' thought Cecil, 'it's "people" now, is it? Only here five minutes and she thinks she's a whole species.' But he put on his nicest smile and said, 'I'm ssso sssorry to have ssscared you. I'm Sssesssil the ssserpent, and I wanted to sssay welcome to thisss Garden of Eden.'

'Well, that's very kind of you, I'm sure,' said Eve. 'No offence meant.'

'None taken,' said Cecil. 'Have you sssampled sssome of the delicasssiesss around here? Sssome of the fruit is sssimply ssscrumptiousss – essspecially that tree in the sssentre of the garden.'

'Oh,' said Eve, 'God said we mustn't eat from it or we'll die.'

'Why,' said Cecil, 'that'sss sssilly! Sssmall-minded sssensssorship! God doesssn't want you to be wise like him, that'sss all.'

Eve was interested. 'You mean,' she asked, 'that if I eat that, I'll be as wise as God?'

'Sssertain as sssunshine in Ssseptember!' answered Cecil. 'Try it – itsss sssensssational!'

Well, the fruit looked tempting – round, plump, and probably juicy, and Eve thought that to be as wise as God would be wonderful. So she took the fruit and ate it. Just then her husband Adam came along and really blew his top. 'You haven't eaten that, have you?' he said.

'Of course I have,' said Eve. 'I knew God was only trying to frighten us – here, have some.' Adam hesitated a moment, and then took the fruit and bit into it. It certainly was lovely. Just as he was enjoying it, Eve shrieked at him so that he nearly swallowed the pips.

'You haven't got any clothes on!'

'What!' exclaimed Adam, and got very embarrassed. Then he looked at Eve and said, 'Neither have you.'

Now the silly thing is they'd never had any clothes on, but they just hadn't bothered about it until they ate the fruit. But now, for some strange reason, they were rushing round the garden trying to find leaves to cover themselves with. Cecil hadn't had such a good time since he was created. He just laughed and laughed until his sides hurt – and he hadn't got any hands to hold them with!

Then he heard the sound of God's voice: 'Adam, where are you?' Adam and Eve were nowhere to be found, but were hiding from God because they were embarrassed. Eventually, God found them and asked, 'What's going on? have you eaten from that tree?'

'It's not my fault,' babbled Adam. 'The woman made me do it.'

'Oh, that's right,' said God, 'blame the woman for it. After all, you might as well start as you mean to go on!'

Then Eve said, 'Don't blame me – Cecil made me do it!'

'What?' said God, 'Cecil the Serpent? But you're supposed to be better and more intelligent than he is.'

'Huh!' thought Cecil. 'That shows what *you* know!'

'Well,' said God, 'that's torn it! I hoped you'd all work together – people, animals, everything – but you're quarrelling and blaming one another right at the start. Life's obviously going to be difficult, and painful, and people and animals will be fighting one another, all because you couldn't just live together the way I wanted. Well, you can get out of this garden, for a start. Go and work for your livings. And as for you,' he said to Cecil, 'since you seem to enjoy saying s's, I'll fix it so that that's all you *do* say from now on.'

'Sssssssssss!' said Cecil – partly because he was angry, and partly because he couldn't say anything else. He was so embarrassed that he just lay down on his stomach and crawled away. And that's how he has been ever since. Men, women and animals carry on fighting and blaming one another, and no one ever wants to admit being wrong.

No wonder we make ourselves unhappy!

Based on Genesis 3

Let's Chat

Do we sometimes blame others
when it's really our fault?

We're Sad

Please forgive us, God,
when we blame others
for what we have done.
Help us to be more caring,
and more honest.

We're Glad

Thank you, God,
for not giving up on us,
even when we give up on you.
Thank you for calling us,
and helping us to accept
our responsibilities.

Let's Pray for People

Loving God,
this is sometimes an unhappy world,
and sometimes people and animals get hurt.
We pray for people who are ill, or in pain;
people who are poor,
people who have no homes.
Help them to know that you haven't given up.
Help *us* to *show* them that.

Rabbles and Babbles

A long, long time ago, in a land called Shinar, some people had what they thought was a great idea. They were convinced that nothing was impossible for them. They believed that all they had to do was work together, and they could do anything. Now at that time, everybody spoke the same language, so working together should have been fairly easy. 'Why,' said Barnaby (who was a nice person but not as bright as he thought he was) 'with our combined knowledge and skills, we could climb right up to heaven!'

Barnaby's friend, Johnny, wasn't so sure. 'To begin with,' he said, 'how do you know exactly where heaven is? Things might be a lot more complicated than you think.'

'Oh, don't be stupid!' scoffed Barnaby. 'Heaven's got to be up there; it's not down here, so that's the only place left. And where do you think all that light comes from?'

'I know it looks that easy,' said Johnny, 'but things might not be quite as they seem.'

Barnaby was impatient, and might have called Johnny a name like 'philosopher', but it hadn't been invented. So he just said, 'Look, it's very simple. What you see is what there is. Don't make things complicated by asking unnecessary questions. This is earth, and heaven's up there. That's how it looks, and that's how it is.'

Johnny didn't like arguing with Barnaby, because he always felt so inferior; Barnaby seemed to know so much, and to be so confident, and Johnny always ended up feeling silly. Still, he couldn't resist saying, 'Perhaps God doesn't want us to climb up to heaven – if that's where it is. Perhaps that's why we can't see it.'

Barnaby thought this was the silliest idea Johnny had had so far. 'Of course God wants us to do it!' he said, scornfully. 'Would he have made us so wonderfully clever, and taught us how to build towers and things if he didn't want us to do it?'

Johnny opened his mouth to ask another question, but Barnaby held up his hand. 'No more!' he said. 'We have a duty to use all the knowledge we have. That's what God expects. So whatever we're capable of doing must be right.'

Johnny thought, 'I'm capable of punching you on the nose, but it wouldn't be right to do it!' But he didn't say that, because he knew Barnaby would have an answer. Barnaby always did!

So everyone set to work – everyone except Johnny and Barnaby, that is. Johnny didn't join in because he thought it was wrong, and Barnaby didn't do any work because he thought he was too important. 'I'm an ideas man,' he used to say. 'I must save my creative energy, and let less important people do the actual work.'

Surprisingly, most of the other people joined in. They were deeply impressed by Barnaby's confidence, and thought Johnny was a very silly man. So the diggers dug the foundations, and the stone masons got the stones ready and started building while the carpenters put in the beams to support the wooden staircase. They were really excited about getting to heaven, and they worked terribly hard every day.

God wasn't happy about it, though. He hadn't put people on earth so that they could spend all their time trying to get back to heaven! He could see what was really happening, and he didn't like it. The people who were building the tower were so obsessed with it that they forgot about everything else. They never played with their children, or looked after their elderly relations. They started to think that the tower was all that mattered; so anybody who wasn't strong enough to work on it was ignored. A lot of people were unhappy, because they weren't wanted, and of course if anyone was ill, and couldn't work, nobody had time to look after them. Some people even died from neglect. All the workers were interested in doing was trying to get to heaven! So God got very angry. 'I'm going to teach them a lesson,' he thought, 'and give them something else to think about.'

So it was that, one morning, Barnaby got up and went out as usual to find an unpleasant surprise awaiting him. He'd have known about it earlier if he'd listened to his wife that morning, but he never did that – he just used to get up and rush straight out to see how the tower was getting on. This particular morning, as he got near to the tower, he heard the most amazing sound – a loud babbling of lots of people all shouting at one another at the tops of their voices. So Barnaby went up and tried to silence them, but he had to get a whistle and blow it before they noticed him. When they did, he started telling them off.

'You're supposed to be building this tower,' he shouted at them, 'not gossiping amongst yourselves – now get on with it!'

Barnaby couldn't understand why the people were looking at him in such a strange, bewildered way. Then the foreman came up and spoke to him, and it was Barnaby's turn to look amazed. He couldn't understand anything the foreman was saying. 'What's the matter with you?' he yelled at the foreman. 'Talk properly so that I can understand you.'

The foreman couldn't understand a word Barnaby was saying, and realised that Barnaby couldn't understand him, either, but he thought it was all Barnaby's fault. Barnaby seemed to be making some very strange noises indeed. So the foreman tried again – but louder. Barnaby still couldn't understand and he shouted back – louder still. Then all the others joined in, and before long everyone was shouting at everyone else, and nobody was listening – even if they had been able to understand!

You know what had happened, don't you? They were all speaking different languages! Everything everybody said made sense – but only to them! No one could understand anybody else at all!

So the tower never got finished.

And it won't be. God is still trying to teach us that heaven isn't in the sky; the way to find heaven is to care about other people, and learn to understand each other.

And all this time later, we're still not very good at it!

Based on Genesis 11:1-9

Let's Chat

We all like to think we're important, don't we?
What ways can we find
of making others feel important?

We're Sad

Sometimes we think we're more important
than anyone else in the world.
Then it ends up with us all shouting at each other
and nobody listening to anyone else.
We're sorry, God.
Please teach us to be good listeners.

We're Glad

Loving God,
everyone matters to you.
We don't need to work at it.
You don't mind if we're not clever.
You just love us, as we are.
Thank you, God.

Let's Pray for People

We pray for people who get forgotten,
people who are in trouble but don't get noticed;
people whose voices get lost
in all the noise others are making.
Please, God, help us to hear them,
so that we can show them
how important they really are.

God's Incredible Promise

Abraham and Sarah were quite old, and lived in a country called Haran. Because they were so old, they were a little bit surprised – well, no, actually they were absolutely flabbergasted – when God said, 'I want you to leave Haran and go to a new place, and I'm going to use you to start off a whole new nation.'

Now, Abraham could have said, 'Children? At our age? Pull the other one, God.' But he didn't, because he thought, 'Well, if God says so, who am I to argue?' And he and Sarah packed up all their things and set off. Now that may seem exciting to you, but in those days it was really very brave. They didn't know where they were going, or what they would find, and they had to leave behind a lot of friends, and all kinds of things they loved. But Abraham said, 'If God's got a plan in mind, we'll just have to trust him.'

Abraham and Sarah had some wonderful adventures on the journey – and some pretty terrifying ones as well – but we haven't got all week, so I'm just going to tell you some parts of the story. The rest of it's in the Bible if you want to read it. They went to Egypt, and had a look around, but being tourists wasn't as easy then as it is now, and they didn't stay all that long. So they carried on moving from place to place, sometimes being baked by the sun, at others being threatened by wild animals and robbers, and all the time a niggling little voice at the back of their minds kept saying, 'How can God give us children when we're so old? If he doesn't get on with it, he'll be too late.' Most of the time, they believed God but they did have their doubts – it's only natural, really. They even tried to hurry God along a few times and take the occasional short cut, but it didn't work. God knew what he was doing, which was a good thing because Sarah and Abraham sometimes didn't!

After more than twenty years of this, most of us would have been beginning to give up hope, and Abraham, to be honest, was getting a bit doubtful, and then God spoke to him. 'You and I have a special friendship,' said God, 'and because of that I'm going to make a great nation from you. Your part of it is to trust me.'

Abraham actually thought this was quite amusing. 'Me, a father, at a hundred years old?' he said, (actually he was ninety-nine but at that age who's counting?), 'and Sarah's nearly ninety.' But God was quite insistent that they would have a child, and lots and lots of great-grandchildren.

Then one day some strangers arrived. Abraham and Sarah didn't know that the men were really angels, but anyway they were good hosts and gave them some food. Abraham sat with the visitors while they were eating outside the tent, and one of them asked, 'Where's your wife?'

'She's in the tent,' said Abraham. Actually, she was standing in the doorway listening.

'I'll come back next year,' said the man, 'and you can show me your son.'

Sarah laughed at that. 'Me?' she thought. 'Ninety years old, and with a body that's seen better days – don't be daft!'

The man turned to Abraham and said, 'Why did your wife laugh just now?'

'What me?' replied Sarah, from the doorway, 'I didn't laugh – oh goodness me no! I wouldn't be so rude as that. It must have been a passing bird – the ones round here have a very strange mating call, you know.'

'Oh no', said the man. 'You laughed all right!'

Sarah was embarrassed, and went back into the tent and pretended to be very busy. Then, for a while, she and Abraham forgot about the visitors and the silly conversations, because they had other things to think about. Abraham's friendship with God was really getting interesting – he even knew God well enough to argue with him and try to change his mind. And most people wouldn't dare to talk to God like that!

As the year went on, Abraham said to Sarah, 'You know, I think you're putting on weight.'

'Don't be silly!' said Sarah, but secretly she wondered about it. They were doing a lot of walking, and life was quite hard, but even with all the exercise she kept on getting bigger. Can you imagine what it was?

One day, she said to Abraham, 'I could really do with a date and onion sandwich.'

'A what!' said Abraham.

'A date and onion sandwich,' said Sarah, 'with boiled potatoes and custard for afters.'

Over the next few months, it got worse. Sarah would get up in the middle of the night to raid the larder. When she started eating pomegranates in a mustard-and-mint sauce, Abraham realised what it was.

'You're pregnant!' he said. 'How wonderful!'

At first Sarah didn't believe him, but gradually as time went on she realised that it was true. Eventually, she had a son. It was the talk of the neighbourhood! A beautiful, bonny bouncing boy, whom she and Abraham decided to call Isaac. All the neighbours came to have a look, and the travelling salesmen who passed by on their camels carried the news all over the place. 'Honestly,' they used to say, 'a baby boy – his dad's a hundred years old and his mum's ninety.'

'Well!' said one of their customers, 'carpets are one thing – but I'm not buying that!'

Sarah and Abraham could hardly believe it, either, but they were wonderfully happy. God had kept his promise.

'It just goes to show,' said Abraham one evening, 'that faith can move mountains.'

Sarah looked up from feeding Isaac. 'Look,' she said, 'I know this is pretty spectacular, but don't go over the top!'

Based on Genesis 12-21

Let's Chat

How do you think Abraham and Sarah felt,
waiting all that time
for God to keep his promise?

We're Sad

Sometimes, God, we don't trust you enough.
Most times, come to think of it!
We think you've forgotten, or got it wrong.
We're sorry for being impatient.
Please help us to trust you more.

We're Glad

Sometimes, wonderful things happen
just when we least expect them.
Sick people get better,
enemies make friends.
Thank you, God, for knowing best,
and for always being here.

Let's Pray for People

Some people are desperate.
They think nobody cares about them;
they think there's no hope of anything better.
Please, God, help them to learn to trust you.
Help us to show them that we care,
and that you care,
and to give them hope.

DON'T ASK ME!

Moses was having a nice quiet life. The rest of the Hebrew people were terribly unhappy, because they were slaves in Egypt, but Moses had escaped and he was working as a shepherd. Apart from chasing the odd wolf away, life didn't get very exciting; he just walked from place to place finding grass for the sheep to eat. Mind you, that was hard work, but Moses never complained because most of the time it was safe, even if it was a little boring.

One day, he was out minding the sheep when he noticed something strange. A bush nearby seemed to be on fire, except that it wasn't going all black and shrivelled the way bushes normally do when they burn. So he thought he'd take a closer look. Then he had the shock of his life – he heard a voice.

'Hey! Moses!'

'What!' exclaimed Moses, looking all round. 'Where did that come from?'

'I'm over here!' said the voice.

Surely, it couldn't be the bush talking, could it? It was really scary! Moses was about to run away when the voice came again.

'Come over here, Moses. I want to talk to you. But take your shoes off, first, because this is holy ground.'

Holy ground! Of course! It was God who was speaking. Mind you, it might have been better if it had been the bush; when God gives people visions he usually has a job for them to do! Moses did as he was told; he took off his shoes and went closer.

'That's better,' said God. 'Now we can talk properly. I've been watching what's been going on in Egypt.'

'Lucky you,' thought Moses. 'I haven't seen a cabaret dancer in years.' But that wasn't what God was talking about. God was very unhappy about the way the Hebrew slaves were being treated, and had decided to set them free. Moses got worried.

'I hope you're not going to ask me to get involved in politics,' he said, 'because I don't think it mixes with religion.'

'Oh, not *that* excuse again!' said God. 'If you had any idea how often I've heard that! Look, people are suffering, and I want to do something about it. And you're going to help me.' This was getting a bit heavy, and Moses really felt he would prefer to talk to the bush, but it wasn't to be. Then he heard the words he'd been dreading.

'You're to go and see Pharaoh,' said God, 'and tell him to let the people go.'

'Go and see who? And tell him what?' squeaked Moses, who was very frightened by now. 'I can't do that! It's all right for you, but I have to live in this world! Anyway, you need a good orator – an experienced politician. I just know what'll happen when I get in front of the king: I'll get all tongue tied – that's if he doesn't cut it out first.'

God wasn't going to listen to that kind of talk. 'Come on, Moses,' he said. 'Trust me. I'll be right with you the whole time.'

Things weren't going Moses' way. So he decided to try another approach. He put on his most reasonable and worldly-wise voice – a bit like a politician who's being given a hard time by an interviewer on the radio. 'Well of course, God, the reality is,' he said, 'that these people have never heard of you. They've been in slavery all their lives, and I'm afraid we need to face up to the situation as it really is – they've forgotten you. I mean, what am I going to say if they ask who you are? Have you got a name?'

God wasn't falling for that. 'Oh no you don't, Moses!' he said. 'You can't put a label on me, like a plant or an animal. I'm greater than any name you could think of. *I* decide who and what I am, and I will be whoever I choose – you go to the slaves and tell them that! And say that I'm going to set them free!'

Moses was getting desperate by now, and he started to repeat himself: 'But no one's going to listen to me!' he wailed. 'I'm a terrible speaker – you ask my wife about that, she'll tell you! No one will take notice of me. Look, I've got a nice home, a lovely wife, and a good, steady job. That's the kind of bloke I am. I'm not into . . .'

The bush seemed to burn more fiercely than before as God interrupted him. 'If you mention politics again, you'll regret it! I care about people – and if you're a friend of mine you will, as well. Stop trying to wheedle out of it and do as I ask.' Then the voice got gentler again. 'Look, Moses, I know you're frightened, but I wouldn't ask you to do it if I wasn't going to back you up. If it makes you feel better, you can take Aaron with you – he can talk.'

'That's true!' said Moses. 'He could talk the hind leg off a camel, could Aaron.'

'That's settled then,' said God. 'Now go and get Aaron, and let's get cracking. We're going to set the people free!'

And that is exactly what they did. But that's a much longer story.

Based on Exodus 3:1-4:17

Let's Chat

Moses had got it made, hadn't he!
He'd got a nice job, a wife and a home.
He didn't think that other people's troubles
were any of his business.

We're Sad

We're sorry, God.
Sometimes we say, 'I can't'
when we mean 'I won't'.
When people are in trouble,
we make excuses for not helping them.
Show us what we can do,
and help us to trust you.
Oh, and don't take 'No' for an answer!

We're Glad

Thank you, God, for not giving up,
even when we do.
Thank you for helping us
to be good friends to one another.

Let's Pray for People

We know that some people are unhappy,
perhaps because other people are cruel to them,
or because they are poor or ill.
Please show us what we can do to help,
and then give us the faith to do it.

You Can't get Water from a Stone

You remember Moses, don't you? He was the man whom God used to lead the Israelites out of Egypt. The trouble was that the people thought he was going to solve all their problems in one go. They'd been slaves all their lives and they thought that Moses was going to lead them straight out of Egypt into a wonderful place where life would be easy. Just like that. They didn't realise that that isn't the way God usually works. So of course, when they cottoned on, they started moaning. And if you think anyone in your family moans a lot, then you haven't heard anything!

Whatever happened, the people were never satisfied. If there was no breeze, they complained about the heat, and if there was a breeze they whined about sand being blown in their faces. During the day, they moaned about all the stuff they had to carry about with them, and said they wished they'd left some of it behind; and then at night they complained that they hadn't got enough blankets to keep warm!

One day, Moses said to God, 'I'm fed up with this. I never wanted the job in the first place – I told you to find someone else. Why couldn't you have left me alone? I enjoyed being a shepherd.'

'Oh, come on, Moses,' said God, 'don't start all that again. I took you from being the leader of a few sheep and made you the leader of a nation.'

'I'd have preferred the sheep,' said Moses. 'On the whole they were probably more intelligent than this lot. And they never moaned at me.'

'That goes with the job,' God answered. 'If you want to be a great leader, you've got to be able to cope with that.'

'But I *don't* want to be a great leader,' said Moses, in despair. 'I was happy as a shepherd, minding the sheep and my own business.'

'Were you?' asked God. 'I don't think so. You knew that your brother and sister and all your people, were slaves and were being ill treated – and you wanted to do something about it. You just didn't think you were capable of it.'

'And I'm not!' Moses insisted.

'I know you're not,' said God, 'but I am. And all you need to do is trust me. Anyway, stop arguing because you've got visitors and they don't look very happy.'

Moses looked round and, sure enough, an angry looking crowd were approaching, and leading them was the chief agitator.

'Oh, no!' said Moses. 'It's that Simon character. He's been making trouble ever since we left Egypt. I suppose he's found something else to moan about.'

'Hey, Moses! shouted Simon. 'We want a word with you. We're thirsty.'

'Well, stop shouting, then,' said Moses, 'or you'll make it worse.'

Simon didn't like that at all. 'Don't you get clever with me,' he snarled at Moses. 'We're all fed up with you and your high and mighty ways.'

'Look,' said Moses, 'I told you we'd get to the Promised Land, and we will.'

'When?' asked Simon, aggressively.

'I don't know,' Moses answered.

'This year? Next year? Sometime? Never?' taunted Simon. Then he went on. 'All right, then – where is it?'

'What d'you mean?' asked Moses.

'Good grief!' said Simon. 'He doesn't even understand plain Hebrew. Watch my lips, Water-baby! WHERE IS THE PROMISED LAND?'

'Don't ask me,' said Moses. 'How should I know?'

'How should you know?' yelled Simon. 'You're the one who's leading us there – of course you should know!'

'Don't be idiotic, Simon,' said Moses. 'Do you think I put that pillar of cloud and fire in the sky? God's the one who's leading us, and as long as he knows where we're going that's all that matters.'

'"God"!' said Simon. 'There you go again. You're mad, you are. Just because you start hearing strange voices, you think it's God talking to you – so you drag us all out here following some silly cloud and expect us to die of thirst without complaining! Look, if you've got God on your side, what about a bit of water – that's not much to ask, is it?'

Then all the others started to join in. 'Water!' they kept shouting at Moses. 'We want water.'

After that, Simon really got going, and started winding up the crowd. 'What do we want?' he shouted.

'Water!' they all shouted back.

'When do we want it?'

'Now!'

Things were starting to look very dangerous.

'Okay, God,' said Moses. 'You told me to trust you. Now what do I do?'

'Simple,' said God. 'Get some water out of one of those rocks.'

Moses wondered whether the heat had got to God, as well! 'What!' he answered. 'Get water out of a stone? That's impossible.'

'Look, Moses,' said God, 'I could get blood out of a stone if I wanted to, but water will do for now. Stop arguing and do as I say. Hit one of those rocks with your stick.'

Moses was really angry, and he would rather have hit Simon, but he knew that would not be a good idea, so instead he raised his stick and brought it down as hard as he could on the rock.

'Temper, temper!' scolded Simon. 'That won't get you anywhere.'

He had hardly got the words out when he heard a strange gurgling sound. Then, to everybody's amazement, a tiny crack appeared in the rock, and a trickle of water came out. Simon and his friends ran forward, excitedly, all fighting to get the first drink in case there wasn't enough to go round. Then just as they got to the rock, there was a thunderous crash and the stone face split wide open as a great rush of water came pouring out. Because Simon was closest to it, he was knocked right off his feet, and ended up rolling around in a big puddle of muddy water. Everyone else thought it was really funny, and every time Simon tried to stand up someone pushed him down again. He was very angry. He had wet sand in his clothes, in his shoes, in his hair, in his ears and in his mouth. And it tasted horrible!

'There you are, Simon,' laughed Moses. 'All the water you could want. That'll teach you not to complain.'

But it didn't.

Simon and his friends found lots more to complain about – people like that always do, of course – but I'll have to tell you about that another time.

Based on Exodus 17:2-7

Let's Chat

Sometimes it seems that
if there wasn't anything to complain about
we'd have to invent something!
Come to think of it, we often do!

We're Sad

Please forgive us, God,
for being so silly!
When we've got water we waste it,
then we complain about the shortage.
And after that, we moan about the rain!
Please help us to be sensible, and grateful.

We're Glad

God, you're full of surprises!
Just when we think we know everything,
you show us something new.
Thank you for this wonderful world,
and the exciting things that happen in it!

Let's Pray for People

It's a funny thing, water.
Sometimes we love it, sometimes we hate it!
But we always need it.
In some places people die of thirst,
and some people get ill
because they have to drink dirty water.
Help us to learn to help one another.

A Little Yellow Idol

Moses was up a mountain, praying, and he had been there a very long time. You might ask why Moses had gone up a mountain, and the most obvious answer is that he felt closer to God. In those days, people really thought that God was 'up there'. There were other reasons, though, and I shouldn't be surprised if he went up the mountain partly to get some peace and quiet. It was the only place where he could get away from all the complaining. The people weren't at all happy about being in the desert. They had thought that as soon as they got out of Egypt they would arrive at the Promised Land. God knew better than that, though. He knew they had an awful lot of thinking and learning to do before they got there. And one good way of thinking is to go for a walk. So God took the Israelites for a walk. Of course, it was rather longer than the ones you and I take, but then they had more to think about than we do. Altogether it was going to last for forty years! Now if they'd known that at the beginning, they would *really* have complained! That is, if they had ever set out, of course!

Anyway, they used to moan and grumble at Moses all the time, as though all the trouble was his fault. 'It's all very well,' Moses said to God, 'but I'm not really leading them, am I? You are. And yet they moan at me as though everything was my fault.'

'That's the way it is,' said God. 'They can't see me – and if they could they'd be too frightened to say anything – so they have a go at whoever they think is closest to me. That's how it's always been, and will be for a long time yet. Anyway, you'd better get to work. I've got a few rules to help you all live properly, and I want you to write them down on stone.'

'That's hard work,' said Moses. 'Can't I use clay or something?'

'Stone,' said God, sternly. 'This has got to last.'

Meanwhile, down at the bottom of the mountain, Simon was stirring up trouble. But then, Simon always did. He was the sort of person who would complain about being hungry when he hadn't any food and then criticise the cooking when he got some. He'd always secretly thought that he would be a much better leader than Moses, so that was another reason to keep on saying how useless Moses was. And at this particular moment, he'd got a crowd round him and was having the time of this life!

'We were better off as slaves!' he shouted. 'At least then we had our bed, board and guaranteed employment.'

'Yeah!' shouted everyone, completely forgetting that it wasn't actually *paid* employment!

'Moses is a fool!' Simon cried.

'Yeah!' responded all the people.

'Couldn't find his way along a straight line if it was signposted!' roared Simon.

'Yeah!' the people shouted, and then went all quiet and embarrassed because of course they should have shouted 'No'!

'How much longer are we going to go on following him?' asked Simon.

'Well, actually, I hate to correct you, but I think in theory we're following God,' said a voice.

Simon snorted. 'Oh really, Levi – trust you to be fussy!' he said, 'and must you carry those silly books around all the time?'

Then Simon had an idea.

'That's it!' he said. 'We need a different God – one we can see.'

'I would counsel extreme caution,' said Levi, wagging a learned finger at Simon. 'You see, from a theological point of view . . .'

'Oh do shut up!' said Simon. 'We don't want any of that theology stuff – just gets in the way, that does.' Then he turned to Aaron. 'Well, you're Moses' brother, aren't you? What are you going to do about it?'

Aaron was very frightened. He could see the crowd were really worked up and he thought they might get completely out of hand. So he thought to himself, 'It wouldn't do any harm – just to calm things down until Moses gets back.' Then out loud, he said, 'All right – collect all the gold you can – people's earrings, bangles, bracelets, anything at all that's made of gold. While that's happening, I want two volunteers to help me make a mould. You and you will do.'

Up at the mountain top, God said to Moses, 'I think you'd better get back down there. They're getting out of hand.'

'Oh, Aaron will handle it,' said Moses, who didn't really want to go back down yet.

'That's what you think!' said God. 'Go on, before I help you on your way. And don't forget to take the commandments with you.'

So Moses went back down the mountain, which took a very long time because he wasn't as young as he used to be and the stone plaques were jolly heavy. When he got near the bottom he couldn't believe his eyes! All the people were singing and dancing and having a real party, and in the middle was this strange looking statue which seemed to be a golden calf. Then, to his horror, he saw people bowing down and praying to it as though it were a god. He hurried down to where they were, and saw Aaron – his own brother – leading it all. Moses was so angry that he threw the stones down on the ground and smashed them. Oh dear. God wouldn't be happy about that!

'Hey! Aaron!' he shouted. 'What's that thing?'

Aaron was frightened. 'Oh – well – er – it was the funniest thing,' he babbled. 'You'll laugh when I tell you.'

Moses didn't laugh.

'Well we just put our gold on the fire,' said Aaron, 'and out came this calf.'

Now you know and I know that it wasn't like that – Aaron gave it a lot of help!

'I'm not swallowing that,' said Moses. 'But *you* are.'

With that, Moses strode up to the altar, and all the people went very quiet when he picked up the idol and started grinding it down. It took him a long time, but no one moved. They were wondering what Moses was going to do.

When the calf was just a heap of gold dust, Moses sent for some water, and poured out a cup for everyone present. Then he sprinkled the gold dust on the water.

'There you are,' he said. 'Drink it!'

The people were horrified. 'He doesn't mean it!' they said.

'Oh yes I do,' said Moses. 'If that thing was a god then it must be full of life and goodness. Now you can find out.'

And Moses made them drink every drop! They found out that it wasn't good at all – it was just a load of metal filings.

'Right,' said Moses, 'you can think about that while I'm gone. Thanks to you, I've got to do all that writing again.'

And with that, Moses set off back up the mountain.

Simon didn't say anything, for a very long time. That was partly because he was so ashamed.

But it was mainly because his throat was sore.

Based on Exodus 32:1-24

Let's Chat

Having fun is important,
but do toys, video games or television
take up too much of our lives?

We're Sad

Sometimes, God, we ignore people
because we're so busy
watching television, or playing.
We're sorry that some things
have become too important to us.
Help us to learn what really matters.

We're Glad

Thank you, God,
for the good things we have,
and especially for our family and our friends.
Help us to enjoy everything you give to us,
and always to put you and people first.

Let's Pray for People

Some people are unhappy
because they haven't got enough.
Other people are unhappy
because they worship money, or possessions.
Please, God, teach us all to love each other
and to share the things that are really important.

THE DONKEY'S TALE

I'm going to tell you a story, but you mustn't let on that it was I who told you. Why? Because we donkeys aren't supposed to know what's going on. It's a great life, being a donkey. Humans always think that they're the only ones who understand anything. So they talk about things in front of us and think it doesn't matter. Let me give you a tip: if you've got any secrets, don't talk about them in front of donkeys, because we've got long ears.

Anyway, I used to work for a man called Balaam. Yes, I know it's a funny name, but most people knew better than to laugh at it because it was said that Balaam could put a curse on you if he wanted to. Once he put a curse on his next door neighbour – all over a misunderstanding. His neighbour used to call him Bally, and one day when he was talking about him somebody asked, 'Bally Who?' and everyone laughed. Balaam thought they were laughing at him and put a curse on his neighbour so that all his hair fell out. So now you know. Don't laugh at people with silly names. In any case, names like Samantha and Alan would have sounded pretty silly in those days . . .

Now where was I? Oh yes – about Balaam. Well, I was standing in my usual place outside the window one day when I saw some visitors coming. I knew who they were straight away. I can tell the king's servants a mile off – all posh clothes and no brains. They told Balaam the king was frightened because the Israelite army were on the way and looked as though they were going to invade. He wanted Balaam to put a curse on the army because he thought it would stop them.

Balaam sent them away with a flea in their ear. 'I don't believe God wants me to do that,' he said. They'd hardly disappeared over the horizon when another lot arrived. I could tell they were even higher officials than the last lot – posher clothes and even less brains. They were really having a go at Balaam. 'Can't you just come along and say what the king wants?' they asked. 'You don't have to mean it, just keep the old so-and-so happy so that we can get a bit of peace.' Well, Balaam kept on saying no, but eventually they got to him, and for the sake of peace and quiet he decided to go with them.

I could have told him that this wasn't a good idea, but he wouldn't have listened. You see, humans have small ears and big mouths – that's their problem. Now if you look at a donkey, you'll find that our ears are bigger than our mouths which is the right way round. We listen a lot, but we say very little. And I knew we were heading for trouble.

Sure enough, we hadn't got very far when we hit a road block. And I don't mean any old road block. None of your silly poles across the road; this was an angel – ten feet tall, shining like a hoarding in Piccadilly Circus.

So of course I did the sensible thing – I turned off into a field. Balaam went mad at me. He kicked, he shouted – and the language!

I knew what the trouble was – Balaam's eyes are even smaller than his ears, and he couldn't see a ten-foot, digitally illuminated angel when it was right in front of him. I thought about telling him to open his silly eyes, but humans get so jealous of animals talking that I decided to keep mum.

It didn't help, though, because we soon had the angel in front of us again, and this time there was nowhere to turn off. I tried to get through between the angel and the wall, but Balaam's foot got scraped against the stones, and he yelled like mad. That's humans for you. They can drive nails into our feet, to fix shoes on, but if we so much as step on theirs they yell and shout fit to bust!

By the next time I saw the angel, I'd had enough and I sat down. Balaam started hitting me and kicking me, and I decided that was it. Like it or not, he was going to hear me talk.

'Are you potty?' I asked him. 'All these years I've been a good donkey to you – do you think I'd do this for no reason?'

Of course, he looked more carefully then – and he saw it too. The angel wasn't very happy. 'What do you mean by being cruel to a poor dumb animal?' he said. I wasn't sure that I liked the 'dumb' bit, but it's not often you get an angel on your side so I didn't complain.

The angel went on, 'If it hadn't been for that donkey of yours you'd be dead by now.' Balaam was full of apologies, of course, and promised never to ill-treat me again. I'll believe that when I see it! Then he tried to turn me round and go home, but the angel stopped him.

'Carry on with your journey,' said the angel, 'but just be careful only to tell the king the truth – even if he doesn't like it.'

From what I gather, things got a bit silly after that, with Balaam refusing to put a curse on the kings' enemies and the king trying to persuade him to do it.

Eventually, the king realised it wasn't going to work and told Balaam to go home without any pay.

Balaam was furious at that. 'All this way,' he said, 'and then he refused to pay me just because I didn't say what he wanted me to. What do you think of that?'

Who? Me? Oh no. I know which side my bread's buttered. I kept quiet. And kept walking.

Based on Numbers 22-24

Let's Chat

Sometimes, telling the truth
can make us unpopular.
But those are the times when
it's most important to be truthful.

We're Sad

Loving God, please forgive us.
It's not always easy to be honest.
Then again, sometimes we're honest
in the wrong way, and we hurt people.
Help us to tell the truth,
and to be kind as well.

We're Glad

Thank you, God,
for people who are truthful to us
even when it's difficult.
It's good to have friends who care
enough to be honest with us.

Let's Pray for People

We pray for people
who have difficult jobs to do:
people who have to give advice
or to take decisions
which others might not like.
Please, God, help them to be honest,
to do and say what they know to be right.

APPEARANCES CAN BE DECEPTIVE

God had a dangerous job for Samuel. Saul, the king of Israel, was making a pretty horrendous mess of things and had to be replaced.

'It's no good keeping on fretting about Saul,' God said to Samuel. 'If he lived for a million years – and I've no intention of letting him – he still wouldn't make a good king.'

'What are you going to do, then?' Samuel asked.

'What *we* are going to do,' said God, 'is anoint a new king.'

'What!' said Samuel. 'While Saul's still alive? Oh, no! I might be religious, but I'm not potty – Saul will feed me to the vultures if I do a thing like that.'

'Oh, do stop going on like that, Samuel,' said God. 'I'm not asking for your opinion about it; I'm telling you what's going to happen. I'm the one who makes the decisions round here, remember?'

'Sorry, God,' said Samuel. 'I suppose you're right as usual.'

'What do you mean, *as usual?*' asked God, indignantly. 'I'm right, *as always* – and there's no "I suppose" about it.'

'No, of course, God. Sorry God,' said Samuel in an embarrassed sort of voice. 'How do you want me to do it, then?'

'Go and see old Jesse, the sheep farmer at Bethlehem,' answered God. 'One of his sons is going to be king. He won't take over yet, but I want him to be anointed so that he's ready.'

'Bethlehem?' said Samuel, incredulously. 'Since when did anything remotely important happen in Bethlehem?'

'My Word!' God answered. 'You ain't seen nothin' yet!'

'Pardon?' asked Samuel.

'Never mind,' answered God. 'That's one of my favourite quotations, but I'm afraid it's after your time.'

Samuel mopped his forehead with his sleeve. 'Can we just get back to this Bethlehem thing?' he asked. 'I can't keep up with this conversation.'

'Just do as I say,' said God. 'Go to Jesse's place in Bethlehem. You can say you've come to hold a special service of thanksgiving, and that you need to see the whole family. I'll tell you which one you're to anoint as king.'

Well,' said Samuel, dolefully, 'I know I shouldn't say this but I really hope you know what you're doing, because if Saul finds out what we've done, one of us is going to get killed. And since you're immortal, I've got a pretty good idea who it will be.'

So it was that Samuel turned up at Jesse's house one afternoon.

'Hello, hello, hello,' called Jesse. 'It's good old Sam the prophet man! Should I be pleased to see you, or have you come with some message of doom for us all?'

Samuel sighed to himself. It was clearly going to be one of those days.

'Look Jesse,' he said. 'I just say what God's given me to say, so if you want to moan at anybody, you'd better talk to *him*.'

'Silly bloke – can't take a joke!' said Jesse, and Samuel cringed. It really was going to be one of those days! The trouble was that Jesse fancied himself as a bit of a poet – why, no one could understand. Samuel had heard that he'd got a son who was good at writing poetry, but if that was so then he obviously didn't get it from his father.

'Look everything's all right. Okay?' Samuel assured Jesse. 'Now send for your family and we'll start the thanksgiving service.'

Jesse answered, 'All right, Sammy, keep your wig on; how'd I know there's something big on?'

'Oh dear,' Samuel thought, 'I'd better get on and do it, or Jesse will put me through it. Good grief! He's got me at it, now.'

Jesse called his sons to join them, and Samuel was really pleased when the first one arrived. 'This must be the one,' he thought. 'I can anoint him and get off home.'

It was true that Eliab looked every inch a king. Tall and strong, and with clear, sparkling eyes, he fitted the part perfectly. Then Samuel heard God speaking to him.

'Don't go by what you see,' he said. 'Appearances can be deceptive. I'll tell you when the right one comes. Don't forget, I don't look at people the way you do. I look at the heart.'

'Oh, I should think his heart's fine,' thought Samuel. 'Healthy looking chap like that.'

'Don't get clever with me,' said God. 'You know what I mean.'

Before Samuel could think of anything else to think, Abinadab arrived, and Jesse introduced him. 'This is my son – another one.'

'I've got to get out of here,' thought Samuel, reaching for his oil.

'Not so fast, Samuel!' said God. This is not the one.'

So Jesse brought the next son over. 'This one is Shammah – takes after his mamma.'

How long was this going to go on for! Still God said no, and still Samuel had to stay there and listen to all that awful rhyme.

Altogether, Jesse presented seven sons to Samuel, but God didn't choose any of them.

'Have you got any more?' Samuel asked Jesse, knowing he'd probably wish he hadn't.

'Yes,' said Jesse. 'Yes, there's another – he's their baby brother.'

'Well, you'd better get him,' sighed Samuel, 'but do me a favour and don't introduce him – let *him* tell me his name.'

'Well, I don't know what you want with him,' said Jesse. 'He's not like the rest – you've looked at the best. I let him earn his keep by caring for the sheep.'

The youngest son came when he was sent for. 'Hello,' he said. 'I'm David. I've heard all about you from my father.'

'Thank the Lord for that!' thought Samuel. 'He's not a jumped up amateur poet!'

David was still quite young, and looked it. His hair probably hadn't seen a comb for days, and he seemed to be trying rather unsuccessfully to grow a beard.

'A nice lad,' thought Samuel, 'but . . .'

'That's the one!' God whispered, excitedly.

Samuel could hardly believe it. 'I thought you said you knew what you were doing,' he said.

'No,' God corrected him. 'You said you hoped I did. I do,

though – he's the one. Well, don't just sit there, get the oil out and do it. Then I'll let you get away from Jesse's silly rhymes.'

'It's a deal!' thought Samuel. And there and then, he took out his horn of oil and poured some over David's head.

'That's it,' he said to Jesse. 'Now remember: don't tell Saul what I've done, or I'll be on the run. Oh, no! I've got to get out of here, before it gets me completely!'

With that, Samuel set off down the road away from Jesse's farm. As he went, he thought, 'David seems a strange choice to me. Still, there's one thing about him – he doesn't write poetry. I wonder which one of them does.'

Based on 1 Samuel 16:1-13

Let's Chat

Do we judge people by appearances?
Have we ever been surprised
when someone has proved us wrong?

We're Sad

We're sorry, God,
for being unfair to people.
We jump to conclusions about them
just because of the way they dress,
or the length of their hair,
or the way they speak.
Please forgive us,
and help us to be fair.

We're Glad

Thank you, God, for wonderful surprises
when people turn out differently
from the way we expect.
Thank you for making the world
so unpredictable!

Let's Pray for People

We know there are people who get badly treated;
sometimes they're bullied because they look different.
Please, God, help them to know
that you love them all,
and help us to control our prejudice.

Choose your Weapons

After David had killed Goliath, King Saul was very nice to him for a time, but it didn't last long. Saul wasn't a good king; in fact he was a bad one. And when the wrong people are in power it has a strange effect on them. They realise that they can't hold down the job fairly, so they start looking for other ways. And they get very worried when anyone comes along who looks like doing it better.

That's how it was with Saul: he knew he'd done a bad job, but he didn't want to lose it. And when David came along, he thought, 'Now here's someone who could take over if I'm not very careful.' Then the people started to cheer for David more than they ever had for Saul, and things started going from bad to worse. Saul used to get terrible depressions and David, who was a bit of a song writer, used to go and sing to him to cheer him up. The trouble was, though, that that just made Saul feel worse, because he knew that once singers get really popular they can be a lot more powerful than politicians. So hearing David sing didn't exactly do him very much good, and before long David had to run away or Saul would have killed him.

David took a few friends – well, rather a lot actually – and went to live out in the fields and caves, hiding from Saul. It wasn't difficult to hide since no one liked Saul anyway and people were very willing to help David – especially if he sang them his latest release.

In one place where they were staying, David's men got friendly with some shepherds who worked for a man called Nabal. David's men would help look after the sheep, sometimes frighten rustlers away, and generally help out. So when they were getting low on food, David thought, 'I know, I'll ask Nabal for help.' He sent a message to Nabal, saying how well his men got on with the shepherds, and asking if Nabal could perhaps spare a little food.

Now the name 'Nabal' meant 'churlish', and he was! Nabal didn't see why he should help David out. 'Why can't these travellers earn their own keep, and not keep sponging off decent people?' he said crossly to his wife.

'Oh, don't be unfair,' said Abigail, who was really much too nice to be married to an old grouch like Nabal. 'David and his men have been really helpful – and they could have just taken what they wanted without asking, because they're all trained fighters.'

'Shut up, woman!' said Nabal. 'This is men's talk!' And he sent David's men back with a great big 'No!' (Actually, he used a few more words as well, but you won't hear those from me.)

David was furious. In some ways, he and Nabal were alike: they both thought you could solve a problem by thumping someone. 'That jumped up little toad!' he bellowed. 'I'll make him wish he hadn't said that – in fact I'll make him wish he hadn't been born!' David buckled on his sword, and called his men. 'Four hundred of you come with me,' he said. 'The other two hundred had better guard the camp.' Then they rode out to teach Nabal a lesson.

Abigail was very angry with Nabal. 'You wouldn't know a friend if one stood up and bit you, would you!' she screamed at him. 'All this time, David and his men have been around, and have you ever lost a single sheep? No. Have you ever had one tiny complaint from anybody? No. But I'll tell you what you have had, you numbskull. You've had complete security, that's what you've had. No one would dare rob you while David's men are here. And you've had the shearing finished three weeks ahead of time – all because of David – and the first time he asks you for anything, what do you do? Just saying "No" isn't enough for you is it? You have to insult him, wind him up, give him reason to hate you. And any time now they're going to show you what a stupid pig you are! No, sorry – that's unfair – our pigs are relatively intelligent.'

Nabal just sat there and sulked – because that's what his name meant.

'Oh, I give up on you!' said Abigail, in despair. 'I suppose I've got to get you out of trouble again. You men! You open your big mouths, get yourselves into trouble, and then we women have to get you out of it.'

Abigail stormed out. 'Don't just stand there,' she yelled at the farm hands. 'Go and pack. I want meat, grain, fruit, honey, and a few kegs of wine wouldn't come amiss – enough for an army!' Then she saddled up a donkey (not Nabal, another one) and went out to meet David, with the servants following behind with all the presents.

When Abigail saw David's army coming, she got off her donkey and waved at them to stop. Now David and his men were very angry and wanted to get to Nabal's place quickly, but then Abigail was very beautiful and she knew that no man was going to ignore her if she seemed to be upset. So when they had stopped, she went over to David and lay down at his feet. 'I'm sorry, my Lord,' she said, 'Please forgive me.'

Now of course David fell for it straight away.

'I'm sorry about my husband,' Abigail wept. 'He really lives down to his name, that one! Look, I've brought you lots of food and drink, and I want you to know how grateful I am for the way you've looked after my shepherds. You will forgive me, won't you?'

David smiled at Abigail and said, 'Thank God you came to meet me today! It would have been terrible if we'd done anything to upset you – even though that husband of yours certainly deserves it.'

'Oh he does, my Lord, he does!' agreed Abigail, smiling at David and trying to look as fragile as possible. 'But I'd be so unhappy if you were angry.'

'I'm not angry any more,' said David. 'Thank you for your presents. I'm glad we managed to settle this without using weapons.'

'Without weapons?' replied Abigail with a mysterious smile. 'I'm not so sure about that.'

Based on 1 Samuel 25:1-35

Let's Chat

Jesus said, 'Blessed are the peacemakers.'
After all, anyone can pick a quarrel,
but it takes a very special person
to stop one.

We're Sad

We're a lot like David and Nabal, really.
Too often we cause arguments
just because our pride has been hurt.
Please God, forgive us;
help us to be more like Abigail
and make peace.

We're Glad

Some people are good at making peace,
calming things down,
helping people understand one another.
Thank you, God, for giving us peacemakers.

Let's Pray for People

We pray for people with quick tempers;
people who are proud and easily insulted;
people who always want their own way.
And we pray for the people they hurt,
who feel afraid, or who lose their dignity.
Please, God, help people to love peace,
and help us learn to be peacemakers.

THEY'RE OUT TO GET ME

Elijah was a prophet, which means that he spoke God's messages to people. Sometimes, he had nice messages to speak, but not always. When God didn't like what someone was doing, he would send Elijah to tell them so. Elijah wasn't always happy about that, especially since the king and queen at that time were really wicked people. They worshipped pretend gods instead of the real one, and they did some horrible things – especially to people who disagreed with them, or upset them for any other reason. So it wasn't very long before Elijah was in trouble.

King Ahab and Queen Jezebel had committed some dreadful crimes, but they still thought that Elijah should be nice to them. They thought that religious people shouldn't tell them they had done wrong. 'Don't mix religion and politics,' they used to say. They actually believed they could do as they liked and God didn't mind – just because they were the nation's leaders! Silly people! Anyway, one day Queen Jezebel sent a note to Elijah saying, 'I'm fed up with you criticising me. I've told you to stop and you haven't. So now I'm going to get you for it.'

Well, Elijah didn't hang around to find out whether she meant it. He packed up his bags, picked up his feet and ran like a hare with a fox on its tail until he came to a cave in the mountains. 'Here's a good place to hide,' he thought.

Just as Elijah was getting the cave ship-shape for the night, he heard God speaking to him. 'Elijah,' said God, 'what are you doing here?'

'I'm hiding,' said Elijah. 'Everyone has turned against you. They've torn down all the churches and killed all the holy people. I'm the only one left who still loves you, and now they're after me!'

'Oh dear!' thought God, 'another silly man who thinks he's the only one who's right.' Then he spoke to Elijah again.

'Elijah, I want you to go and stand at the front of the cave.'

Elijah wondered what was going on, but he wasn't up to arguing with God. So out he went, but as he got outside an enormous wind sprang up and went whistling through the valley. Elijah nearly got blown off the ledge he was standing on. He huddled against the rock and wanted to go back inside the cave, but he knew he had to stay there as God had told him. 'I expect God is going to speak to me in this great strong wind,' he thought. But God was not in the wind.

Soon, the wind stopped and Elijah thought, 'Thank goodness that's over!' Just as he was thinking it, the earth began to shake – just a little at first, but it soon got stronger. And before long everything was rocking and shaking and great big cracks were appearing in the rocks around Elijah. 'Wow!' he thought, as he crouched in a terrified huddle against the mountain, 'God must have something really important to say.' But God wasn't in the earthquake, either.

After the earthquake, Elijah was just getting his breath back when there was a sudden flash and it looked as though the whole world was on fire. Elijah couldn't understand how he survived it; everything seemed to be burning furiously, the trees, the grass – even the sky itself was like a raging inferno. But still God didn't seem to be around. Elijah was very puzzled.

The fire died down and everything went quiet. Elijah waited for whatever was coming next – perhaps a great flood, or a blizzard, or maybe a stampede of wild animals – but nothing happened. Absolute silence. Elijah decided to go back into the cave. Perhaps in the morning he would realise it had all been a dream. Gosh, but it was quiet! It was one of those silences when you get the feeling that something is going to happen. But Elijah was just too tired to bother. So he went back into his cave, and then he heard it. A soft, gentle whisper. A tiny little voice. 'Who's that?' he thought. 'Not one of the queen's men, I hope.' He stood very still and listened, and he heard it again. Then he realised it was God. Well, fancy that! All that spectacular noise and terrifying power, where any normal person would have expected God to be speaking, and all the time Elijah was supposed to be listening for a tiny little voice!

Elijah was rather scared by all this, and he wrapped his cloak around his head and went back to the cave entrance, peering through the folds of his cloak like a frightened child! Then God spoke again. 'What are you doing here, Elijah? Why aren't you at home?'

'I can't stay there!' said Elijah. 'They've killed all the prophets, broken all your rules – I'm the only one left who cares about you – and now they're out to get me, as well.'

'Don't flatter yourself!' said God, 'You're not the only one who's got it right, by a long way.'

'Well it feels that way,' said Elijah, sulkily.

'Go back,' said God. 'You'll find I've got quite a lot of friends out there. Some of them are going to take over as great leaders, and the evil people won't have the power any more. So you've nothing to be afraid of. "Only one" indeed! There are a good seven thousand more like you – so stop feeling sorry for yourself and go back to join them.'

So Elijah went back. Things didn't change instantly, and Elijah still upset the king and queen by what they called 'interfering in politics', but God was always Elijah's friend and Elijah learnt to trust him. He didn't see fires and earthquakes every day – but he often heard that tiny, whispering voice.

Based on 1 Kings 19:1-18

Let's Chat

We often think like Elijah,
expecting God to be noisy.
Why do we think that noisiness is a sign of power?
We forget that God is so powerful
that he doesn't need to throw his weight around!

We're Sad

Sorry, God!
We're always trying to find you in the wrong places.
You come to us quietly,
you speak to us gently,
and we don't hear,
because our ears are only tuned in to loud noises.

We're Glad

Thank you, God, for being you,
and not who we expect you to be.
Thank you for gentleness,
for silence, for rest.
Thank you for your still, small voice.

Let's Pray for People

Some people's lives are always noisy,
full of rush and bustle.
Help them to see the importance
of quietness and rest.
And help us to live
as though we know it, too!

Elijah's Last Journeys

Elijah and Elisha were friends. Elijah was the chief prophet at the time, and I suppose you might say that Elisha was his apprentice. They spent a lot of time together, and everyone guessed that God would probably ask Elisha to take over sometime.

One day, they both knew that it was going to happen, but they didn't talk about it. Elijah seemed restless. He'd always been a bit of a wanderer, which was no bad thing since God was always sending him to different places to do what prophets do. Then of course, there was that time when he had to run away from Queen Jezebel (anyone in their right mind *would* run away from Queen Jezebel) and he'd been very glad of being so fit. This particular day, though, he *really* seemed to have sand in his underwear!

'I'm going to Bethel,' said Elijah, 'because God wants me to go there. Now you stay here and rest while I'm away.'

'Not on your life!' answered Elisha. 'I want to be around when the action starts; I'm coming with you.'

'Well, all right, then,' grunted Elijah. 'Just make sure you keep up.' And with that he set off at a cracking pace toward Bethel. When they got there, they found a reception committee waiting for them. The Bethel branch of the Prophets' Commission came out to meet them. Some of them took Elisha aside and said, 'Did you know that God's going to take Elijah away, today?'

'Yes, I did know,' said Elisha, 'but don't go talking to him about it, will you.'

Then Elisha sat down on a handy milestone and took his sandals off. 'My life!' he said, 'but can that man walk! I've got blisters where I didn't even know I'd got skin!'

Elijah came up to him and looked down at his feet for a moment. 'You young people!' he said. 'In my day we'd walk twenty miles just to find a drink of water, and think nothing of it at all.'

Elisha would probably have been rude to Elijah, but since

he knew it was their last day together, he just smiled at him. Elijah was really quite a gentle sort underneath, and he smiled back as he said, 'Look, you stay here with these good people. I'm going to go to Jericho.'

'Jericho!' exclaimed Elisha. 'Whatever do you want to go to Jericho for? Nothing exciting ever happens in Jericho. Ever since Joshua brought the walls down, no one's dared throw a decent party in case something collapses. There's really nothing to go to in Jericho.'

Elijah was very patient. 'I'm not going there for a party,' he said. 'I'm going because God's told me to. Anyway, I've already said you can stay here.'

'Not likely!' said Elisha. 'I'm not leaving you today, and if you want to go to Jericho then you can bet your life I'll be there as well.'

So off they set, and Elijah didn't seem the least bit tired but went striding along ahead.

'What's the matter with you?' gasped Elisha. 'You're rushing around like there's no tomorrow.'

'Funny you should say that . . .' replied Elijah. And Elisha wished he hadn't.

When they got to Jericho, what do you think they found? Another reception committee; this time from the Prophets' Commission Department Of Soothsaying. One of the prophets came up to Elisha. 'Sooth! Sooth!' he chanted.

'What d'you mean, "Sooth"?' snapped Elisha, impatiently.

'Sorry, Guv,' said the prophet, 'but I've got to say "Sooth" because I'm a "Sooth" sayer. Did you know that your boss is going to be taken away today?'

'Yes, I did,' said Elisha, 'but don't say anything to him. And don't go yelling "Sooth" in his ear, either – if you know what's good for you.'

'Well!' said the soothsayer. 'I've had my nose bitten off a few times, but that's what I call a mega bite!' And with that, he went off, chuntering to himself.

Elisha sat down and looked mournfully at his feet. 'I've got blisters on my blisters, now!' he groaned.

Elijah came over to where Elisha was sitting. 'Blisters?' he said. 'Oh, don't tell me about blisters. When I was a young prophet . . .'

'All right, all right!' Elisha interrupted. 'I've heard it before: "Up to your neck in muck and . . ."'

'No need to be offensive!' Elijah sniffed. 'Anyway, you can have a rest now, because I'm going to the river Jordan. You wait here.'

'Not on your cotton-picking life!' said Elisha. 'After all this walking, you're going to a nice cool, fresh river, and you think I'm staying here?'

So off they went, and soon they got to the Jordan. That's right – another reception committee. This time it was from the Prophets' Bureau.

One of them came over to Elisha. 'Did you know . . .' he began.

'Oh, don't you start as well!' said Elisha. 'I know he's leaving today, and I'm unhappy enough without you rubbing it in. And talking of rubbing – Oh, my feet!'

'Sorry, I'm sure!' said the man, rather stiffly. Then Elijah came over and said, kindly, 'Sorry about all the walking, but we're about there now. Let's get across that water.'

'How are we going to get across?' asked Elisha.

'No problem,' said Elijah as he took off his cloak and hit the water with it. There, before Elisha's astonished eyes, the water moved to each side and left a nice dry path to walk across. 'Come on,' said Elijah, 'or you'll miss the big moment.'

As they walked, Elijah said, 'Is there anything I can do for you before I go?'

Elisha was still amazed by what Elijah had just done. 'A double portion of your special power wouldn't go amiss!' he said.

'That might be difficult,' said Elijah, 'but I'll tell you what. If you actually see me taken away, then you'll get your wish. So stick with me – I'm going places.'

Elisha did exactly that, until suddenly he saw something bright and terrifying coming towards them. He did his best to stay close to Elijah, but the strange thing came rushing through between them and picked Elijah up. It was a horse and chariot which seemed to be made of fire! Up and up it went, carrying Elijah with it. As Elisha looked up in astonishment, he saw Elijah's cloak coming down from the chariot to land at his feet. He picked it up and put it on.

'That's it!' he thought. 'Elijah's cloak! It's a sign!'

And it was. Elisha became a great prophet, just as Elijah had been.

Based on 2 Kings 2:1-15

Let's Chat

Elijah and Elisha were great friends;
they never let each other down.

We're Sad

We're not always like Elijah and Elisha.
Sometimes we let people down,
and we're not there when they need us.
We're sorry, God.
Help us to be better friends to each other.

We're Glad

God, our friend,
you're always here for us.
Even though we sometimes find it hard
to recognise you,
you never leave us on our own.
Thank you.

Let's Pray for People

Some people don't seem to have any real friends.
They have to get through the hard times
without the help they really need.
Make us alert to other people,
so that we recognise when they're lonely;
then we can be friends to them.

Keep It Simple

Naaman lived in the country of Aram, and was a commander in the king's army. He was a great soldier who had been involved in lots of battles and had the scars to prove it, but when he wasn't soldiering he lived quietly with his wife, Jessica, in their house near the barracks.

Naaman and his army were often sent by the king of Aram to raid Israel and bring back treasure. The king wasn't really such a bad man; kings just thought they could do that kind of thing in those days, and a lot of rulers and politicians still haven't learnt any better now.

Anyway, on one of the raids Naaman brought back a young girl called Anna and gave her to his wife as a slave. Now you might have thought that Anna would hate Naaman and Jessica for that, but she always tried not to. 'After all,' she used to say, 'we've all got to live together and hating them would just make me feel even more unhappy.' So although she missed her home very much, and longed to go back, she always tried to think kindly of Nathan and Jessica.

One day, Anna said to Jessica, 'I hope you won't mind my saying this, my lady, but the commander doesn't seem very well. That nasty rash is getting worse.'

It was true. Nathan had a really uncomfortable skin disease, and it seemed to be spreading, but none of the doctors in Aram could do anything about it. 'I know someone who can, though,' said Anna. 'Send him to Israel to meet the prophet who lives there, and he'll make the commander well again.'

When the king of Aram heard about it he thought it was certainly worth a try, so he sent Naaman to the king of Israel with a letter, saying, 'Please make my army commander better.'

'Oh dear,' groaned the king of Israel. 'He's trying to pick a quarrel with me – how on earth can I make this soldier better?' And he got really frightened, and – well, you know how rumours about royal families spread – before long the whole country was talking about how frightened the king was, and wondering if it meant the end of the monarchy.

'It's true, you know,' someone said in the market place. 'He's so frightened he never goes to sleep any more. What sort of a king is he?'

Standing nearby was a man called Elisha. He was the prophet Anna had meant, but that's the trouble with some people; they think only kings and queens have the answers to anything – so Naaman had been sent to the wrong person! Still, it wasn't too late. Elisha sent a message to the king of Israel, saying, 'Send Naaman to me – I'll help him, and then you can get a good night's sleep.'

So it was that Naaman turned up at Elisha's door. When Elisha opened it, Naaman stood and waited for something spectacular to happen – you know, a flashing light, or something, or perhaps God would zap him and make him fall over. He liked a bit of theatre, did Naaman. But all Elisha said was, 'Oh, it's you. Right. Go and take a dip in the river Jordan. In fact, while you're at it, take seven dips – you've had a long journey. Then you'll get rid of your rash.'

Well! What a letdown! Naaman got back on his horse, and set off for home. He was furious! 'I'm not being made a fool of by any Israelite!' he said, but his servant was actually a lot wiser than he was – which is often the case.

'Why not do it?' the servant asked, 'After all, if he'd asked you to do something difficult you'd have done it, just to get a bit of glory – so why not do something simple?'

It seemed like a good point. Anyway, Naaman was hot and sticky, and covered in dust, so he thought he might just give it a try. He stopped on the river bank and took off his clothes while his servant kept watch. Then he went into the river and ducked under. 'Ugh!' he thought, 'What do they empty into the river around here?' But he didn't want to look like a coward, so he went under seven times, just like he'd been told. Then he got out of the water and started to dry himself. 'There!' he said to his servant. 'Satisfied now? Let's go home before I have to do anything else that's stupid . . . What on earth's the matter with you now?'

His servant was staring at him as though he'd seen a ghost. 'Sir! Sir!' he shouted. 'Your rash has gone!' Naaman looked down, and sure enough, it had! His skin looked fresh and healthy again – almost like a baby's skin.

Naaman went rushing back to see Elisha and say thank you to him. He offered Elisha presents – beautiful clothes, gold and silver – but Elisha wouldn't accept any of them. That wasn't why he had helped Naaman. So Naaman set out for home, and thought what a lot he had learned during his visit to Israel.

When Naaman got home, everybody celebrated. Jessica was overjoyed to see Naaman looking so healthy, and not scratching himself all the time, and Anna was really pleased to see how happy they both were.

Naaman thanked Anna, and he thanked his servant, too. 'I'll never be too proud to do something simple again,' he said. 'Very often, the simplest ideas are really the best ones.'

Based on 2 Kings 5:1-14

Let's Chat

Have you ever been really worried,
and not recognised the answer
because it wasn't complicated enough?

We're Sad

Loving God,
sometimes we're so proud!
Forgive us for being snobbish,
and show us how you work
in simple ways.

We're Glad

Thank you, God,
for the simple things in life:
for smiles, and hugs,
and for friendship.

Let's Pray for People

Let's pray for busy people;
people whose lives are so complicated
that they don't have time for simple beauty,
or for little joys.
Please help us make space in our own lives,
so that we can show how much those things matter.

Walking Through Fire for God

This is a story about three men who lived a long time ago. Their names were Shadrach, Meshach and Abed-nego. Yes, well they would probably have thought that Tom, Dick and Harry were silly names as well. They actually came from Jerusalem, but they couldn't live there because the king of Babylon had conquered Jerusalem and made them slaves. So they lived – yes, you've guessed it – in Babylon.

They weren't too unhappy there, at first. The king – whose name was Nebuchadnezzar – realised they were very clever and thought they might be useful to him. So he gave them a fairly good life. As long as they didn't cause any trouble they would be well looked after.

Everything seemed to go very well, until the king got a little too big for his boots. He made a great big golden statue, which was as tall as three houses put on top of one another. It was so big that he couldn't get it into his back yard, but had it set up in a large open space. Why was it so big? Well, he just thought that bigger meant better, and he wanted to have the biggest statue around. Then, when he'd had it built he decided that it was so wonderful it must be a god, and he told everybody to worship it. That may seem a bit daft to you, but just be thankful they didn't have rock stars or footballers in those days or they might have worshipped something *really* silly . . .

Anyway, the king decided that he was going to have some fun. 'We're going to play musical prayers,' he said. 'And I don't mean we're going to sing hymns. It's a bit like musical chairs but with a difference. As soon as the music starts, you've all got to lie down and pray. And anyone who isn't lying down by the time it stops is out – *permanently!* Do you understand what I mean?'

Some people weren't sure, so the king spelt it out for them. 'Anyone not praying to this wonderful god I've made will be thrown into the burning fiery furnace,' he explained. 'Is that clear enough for you?'

'I think I understand,' said a voice in the crowd. 'You mean we'll be out – *permanently.*'

'Well done,' said the king. 'I do believe you've got it. Now let me see, is everyone here?'

By this time, Shadrach, Meshach and Abed-nego had been made provincial governors over parts of Babylon, so of course the king expected that they'd do exactly as he said. After all, they should be grateful to him when he'd been so kind to them, he thought. They were among the crowd waiting for the music to start. Shadrach turned to his friends and said, 'I don't fancy the burning fiery furnace, but I don't want to bow down and worship that heap of scrap metal, either.'

'Neither do I,' said Meshach. 'It can't be a god – after all, it was made by people, which seems just a little bit the wrong way round to me.'

'It's an ugly brute, anyway,' added Abed-nego. 'How can anyone worship anything as repulsive as that?'

Just then, the trumpets sounded, the drums were beaten, and the horns were blown. Everyone else lay down very quickly, because no one wanted to be last on their feet, but Shadrach, Meshach and Abed-nego were still standing there,

deep in conversation. 'Ooh, look!' cried the King's Personal Private Secretary, who was a really bloodthirsty person and quite mad. 'They're not bowing down! They're not worshipping! They're talking! Ooh, Your Majesty! Can I stoke the fire? Can I pour some oil on it? Go on, Your Majesty! Please let me pour some oil on it. Nasty little forriners – think they can come over here and do as they like! Please let me stoke the furnace, Your Majesty!'

'Oh, do shut up!' said the king, who was really tired of his secretary's sillyness. Then he called out. 'Hey, you three. Didn't you hear the music?'

'Oh, yes – we heard it,' answered Shadrach, 'but if you think we're bowing down to that heap of scrap metal you've got another think coming – Your Majesty.'

The king was hopping mad, and his nasty little secretary was delighted.

'Ooh! Listen to that!' screamed the P. P. S. 'Put 'em in the fire, Your Majesty! Put 'em in the fire! That'll teach 'em a lesson – I'll bet they do as they're told after that! Go on, Your Majesty! Show 'em whose country this is!'

The king was very tempted to put his Personal Private Secretary on the fire as well, but he controlled himself. He didn't really want to do it to Shadrach, Meshach and Abed-nego, either, because he liked them. 'Look, you chaps,' he said, 'why don't you just do it and save us all a lot of grief? You don't have to *mean* it. Just lie down and move your lips, and that will be enough.'

'No' said Shadrach.

'Well, would you just kneel, then?' suggested the king.

'Not likely,' said Meshach.

'Just a quick bow? If we all close our eyes?' begged the king desperately.

'Not on your life!' said Abed-nego.

The P. P. S. was jumping up and down with excitement.

'Go on, Your Majesty. Burn 'em! Coming in here, bringing all their relations with them, eating our food, taking our jobs – put em on the fire, Your Majesty! Put 'em on the fire!'

So, very reluctantly, the king had to order that Shadrach,

Meshach and Abed-nego be tied up and put into the furnace. The P. P. S. had the time of his life, and he kept going to the spy hole to peep in and see if they were burning. Suddenly he came running back towards the king.

'Your Majesty!' he screeched, 'They're walking about. And none of them are burning! Tell 'em to burn, Your Majesty – tell 'em to burn!'

Immediately, the king had the furnace opened, and Shadrach, Meshach and Abed-nego came out. There wasn't so much as a scorched eyebrow between them. The king was thrilled to bits! 'We're not going to worship gold and silver any more,' he said. 'From now on we'll worship God.'

Based on Daniel 3:1-28

Let's Chat

Stories like this aren't as simple as they seem:
don't play with fire!

We're Sad

You don't ask us to walk through fire.
You ask us to do smaller things,
but still we're afraid:
afraid of being laughed at, or losing our friends.
We're sorry, God; help us to be more faithful.

We're Glad

Thank you God, for special people
who have stayed faithful to you,
who have stood up to evil,
and who have made the world a better place.

Let's Pray for People

A lot of people are afraid of doing what is right.
They don't want to seem different,
and they're afraid of looking silly.
Please give them strength;
and when they're people we know,
help us to encourage them by our friendship:
by understanding how they feel,
and by being prepared to join with them
to stand for what is right.

A Camel's Eye View

Allow me to introduce myself. My name's Constance, and I'm a camel – and before anyone says I've got the hump, let me tell them that that joke isn't funny any more. Or not to a camel anyway.

Now, I wouldn't want you to get the wrong idea – I'm not just any ordinary camel. I'm a Bactrian camel, which means I've got breeding. Straight out of the top drawer of four legged Arabian society. Don't think I'm prejudiced, though – some of my best friends are dromedaries. I fully realise that they can't help being different, and I've got nothing against them. Mind you, I wouldn't want one as an in-law, but that's another matter. I suppose I'd better get on with telling you the story. It's about the people who live in my annexe – Caspar, Balthazar and Melchior, otherwise known as the Three Wise Men.

It all began one evening when I was relaxing with my friend Clarissa, chewing away at some very tasty fig leaves. We were just saying that it seemed a lot lighter than usual at that time of night when the three wise men came rushing in, all excited – without even bothering to knock. Apparently there was a big star in the sky and they reckoned it meant a new king had been born. And they had Clarissa and me, and the other camels, saddled up so fast I nearly choked on my fig leaf.

Soon we were plodding across the desert following this star. We had to travel by night, of course, so that we could see it, and rest in the day. I don't mind saying I was not very pleased about that. After all, when did you last hear of a member of the upper classes working the night shift? Then when we worked out where we were going, I began to think something was seriously adrift. It looked to me as though we were heading for Judea.

Now I wasn't happy about that; I'd heard about Judea from other camels I'd met on the trade routes. Apparently the people there weren't too keen on foreigners. More than that, they said their God didn't approve of astrology, so I didn't think they'd exactly welcome us.

Still, the wise men were urging us on and who was I to

argue? Not that it would have done any good, anyway. Humans expect us to understand them, but they never seem to have a clue what we're saying! And they think they're a superior breed!

Anyway, to return to the story, we trailed across the desert following this star. My dears, it was simply frightful! We had to put up with sandstorms, flies and the most obnoxious little sand lizards who seemed to think they had as much right to be there as we did. Really!

Then eventually, we saw the city of Jerusalem ahead, and stopped at the palace. At least that was a reasonable place for a quadruped of my breeding. Caspar knocked on the door, and asked to see the king – chap called Herod.

I don't mind telling you, I didn't like what I saw. Shifty character – couldn't look me straight in the eye.

'Hello, hello, hello,' I thought, 'He's a wrong 'un or I'm an African elephant.'

Well, Herod didn't seem too pleased to hear that another king had been born – and I have to say I had some sympathy – but after he'd done some checking up he sent us along the road to Bethlehem. He asked the wise men to go back when they'd found the baby king and tell him where he was 'so that he could pay his respects', he *said.* And if you believe that, then you will believe anything!

Anyway, I wasn't happy about going to Bethlehem. Bethlehem, my dears, is one of those dreadful little tourist resorts where the common creatures go. Most of the humans ride donkeys – and some even walk! Would you believe it? I could have told Caspar, Melchior and Balthazar that they'd never find a king there. Still, they wouldn't have listened – so off we set.

My dears it was simply ghastly. There were all these crowds of people there, all pushing and jostling one another in the most vulgar way. Then the star stopped and shone down as if to say, 'This is the place'. In went the three wise men – 'wise'? – I like that! And they brought out their presents. You should have seen what they gave the child. Gold – real solid twenty-two carat gold – none of your cheap plate – then some incense, and finally some spice – a particularly smelly variety called myrrh. And to think that all the way along I'd been blaming Clarissa's feet!

That night, I hardly got a wink of sleep. The three wise men were chattering away until the small hours – going on as though they'd had a ringside seat at the gladiators world cup final in Rome! I wanted to say to them, 'It's only a baby – you could have seen one of those at home,' but they wouldn't have listened.

Anyway, eventually they fell asleep and we all got a bit of peace. Then in the morning Caspar said a very strange thing. 'Let's give the palace a miss,' he said. 'An angel told me that Herod's not to be trusted.'

Well, I could have told him that! Anyway, we went home by a different way – and a longer one – and Clarissa's feet haven't been right since.

It's a funny thing, you know, but that baby's been really on my mind. I mean, I thought the whole trip was a disaster – but I just get this niggling feeling that there was more to it than meets the eye.

Oh well – time will tell, I suppose.

Based on Matthew 2:1-12

Let's Chat

What 'stars' do you follow?
Think about your hopes and dreams,
about your ambitions.
What is *really* important to you?

We're Sad

Please forgive us, God,
for wanting so much to be comfortable
that when you call us on a journey
we don't want to go.
Help us to trust you, and to follow you
wherever your 'star' may lead us.

We're Glad

Thank you God,
for not leaving us to do nothing.
Thank you for giving us hopes and dreams,
and thank you for leading us on life's journey.

Let's Pray for People

We pray for people who don't seem
to have any 'stars' to follow:
people to whom nothing seems important enough
for them to take the risk of following it,
and people who are so poor or neglected
that they can't afford the luxury of a 'star'.
Please, God, give all people something to look forward to.

JESUS MAKES MATTHEW RICH

When the Romans invaded Israel, most of the Israelites were very angry about it. They hated the Romans: they hated their religion, they hated their soldiers, their music, their clothes . . . That's how it is when invasions happen. People just hate everything about the invaders.

Some people definitely benefited from the Roman take-over, though, and one of them was Matthew. He was an accountant, and the more money the local traders made the more he could charge them for looking after their accounts. Also, he knew quite a lot of ways of fiddling his own books to cheat his clients, and again the richer they were the more he could do it. So of course, with all the extra trade the soldiers brought, his clients were doing very well and so was he. Then one day the local Roman governor sent for him and said, 'How would you like to collect taxes for me?'

At first, Matthew wasn't any too sure. It was a well-paid job, but then it needed to be. Everyone hated tax collectors who worked for the Romans – they called them traitors.

'That depends,' he said. 'What's in it for me?'

'Whatever you like,' answered the Governor. 'I don't care how much you cheat these people, just as long as you get the taxes in.'

'Sounds good,' said Matthew, thoughtfully, 'but I'm not sure.'

'Well, let me help you make up your mind,' said the Governor – with a smile that was just a little too nice. 'If you work for me, I'll let you keep your head.'

Matthew noticed a very large soldier move a little closer to him and grasp the hilt of his sword. 'Yes, yes, of course, Your Excellency!' Matthew babbled in panic. 'It would be an honour indeed to work for the glorious Roman Empire.'

So, next morning, Matthew was in a different office with a big desk and chair, and with a notice on the outside saying *All Taxes Collected. No credit – No I.O.U.s – No Forged Fivers, Dubious Dollars or Duff Denarii.*

Matthew quickly became very rich, but he found that there was a price to his wealth. When he met his old friend Adam in the street, Adam didn't say hello. 'Hey,' shouted Matthew, 'you blind or something?'

'Not so blind I can't recognise a traitor when I see one!' answered Adam, and kept on walking. That's how things went on – except that they got worse. When Matthew went home after work he found horrible words written on his front door: words like 'Traitor' and 'Filthy Scum'. After the first few days he didn't even bother to wash it off any more, because it just left people room to write something worse. He stopped going out at night, as well – partly because he had no friends to go out with, and partly because it was too dangerous. He had to have armed guards with him the whole time – he couldn't even pop down the road to buy a pomegranate without three big men to keep him company. After a while, he was beginning to wonder whether being so rich was worth it.

One day, he was sitting at his desk having an argument with a taxpayer. 'You're charging too much,' the man was saying.

'Look, smartie pants,' said Matthew sarcastically. 'If you had to do this rotten job you'd charge a lot, too.'

'Oh, hearts and flowers!' replied the other man. 'Some people would be glad to have a job at all, with the way things are going. Ever since this lot took over, *decent* people haven't been able to make an honest living.'

Then a new voice joined in. 'You having a spot of bother, Matthew?'

Matthew looked up and saw Jesus standing there. He'd seen him before, and heard him preach, but he'd always thought the man was a useless, woolly minded romantic. He went around saying there were more important things than money, and Matthew had never been able to understand how he could say that. 'The man's a loser,' he used to say to his friends, 'and a mad one at that.'

Matthew didn't say that any more – and only partly because he hadn't got any friends to say it to. If the truth be told, he was beginning to think the chap had a point. Suddenly, he sat bolt upright in his chair, as though he'd been struck by lightning.

'Tell you what,' he said to his client. 'Why don't we just forget the whole thing?'

'What!' gasped the man, in amazement.

'Go away,' said Matthew. 'Keep your money. I don't know what you see in the lousy stuff anyway! Nothing but trouble, if you ask me.'

The astonished man gathered up his money and left, not waiting for Matthew to change his mind. Matthew turned to Jesus. 'That's it!' he said. 'I've had it with money.'

'Don't blame the money,' said Jesus. 'We all need a bit of that. Your problem is that you're addicted to it – and that's what's wrong. Now if you were with me, you'd never have the chance to get addicted to money – there's never enough of it around!'

Matthew looked at Jesus, and the friends he had with him with their creased clothes and unkempt hair. 'If you don't mind my saying so,' he said, 'you're not exactly a good advert for simple living, are you?'

'Oh, I don't know,' said Jesus. 'No one writes nasty things on *my* front door, because I haven't got one – and I don't have trouble with my tailor, either. I'll tell you what I have got, though. I've got friends. If I fancy a nice comfortable bed for the night, there's always somewhere I can go. And when it comes to money . . .'

'All right!' said Matthew. 'You can start by coming for lunch with me. I've had it with this lousy job!'

When the religious leaders saw where Jesus was going, they were horrified. 'That Jesus fellow always mixes with the wrong people!' they said.

'Well, if you're as good as you think you are,' Jesus answered, 'you don't need me anyway. People who aren't ill don't need doctors.'

As soon as the meal was over, Matthew told his bodyguard, 'I'm resigning. Tell the governor to find someone else.'

'He'll have your head for that!' grumbled the bodyguard.

'Ah,' said Matthew. 'He'll have to find me first, and as of right now I haven't got an address.'

Based on Matthew 9:9-13

Let's Chat

People can be so 'holier-than-thou', can't they!
Do we ever treat people badly
because we disapprove of them?
And does it make us feel good about ourselves?

We're Sad

We're sorry, God, for times when we hurt people
because we think they're bad and we're good.
Teach us never to judge people,
always to remember that things may be
less simple, or obvious, than we think.

We're Glad

Thank you, God,
for forgiving us when we're not as good
as you would like us to be.
Thank you for those wonderful people
who always seem able to be nice to us
even when we don't deserve it.
Help us to be more like them.

Let's Pray for People

We pray for people who think they are good,
and people who think they are bad;
people who judge others,
and people who don't like themselves.
Help them to know your love,
which makes us all truly rich.

Don't Be Stingy!

Jesus wanted to show how generous God is with his love. So he told a story a bit like this one.

Sally was a farmer. Well, I suppose nowadays you'd call her place a small holding, because it was not very large. In those days, though, about the time that Jesus lived, a set-up of that size would be called a farm. She grew quite a lot of different crops, and she always had enough to feed her family and plenty to sell so that they would have some money to buy the things they couldn't grow. Everyone knew what a good farmer Sally was; everyone, that is, except her next door neighbour, Jake.

Jake didn't like waste. He hated seeing anything, no matter how small, not being used as well as possible. Now that's not such a bad thing, up to a point – sensible people don't waste valuable things – but Jake took it to ridiculous extremes. He would lean over the fence, while Sally was working hard in her garden, and say things like, 'You've got to make as much profit as you can, you know,' or, 'You ought to target your resources where they will be most effective.' Sally didn't really understand what all that meant, but she enjoyed her work and it always seemed to provide for her. She liked Jake, as well, even though he was a pain in the posterior most of the time; so she didn't say hurtful things back, but just smiled and nodded – and ignored him!

Sally's crops were doing very well, and one day she said to her husband, Tom, 'I think we should grow our own wheat this year. It's silly that we have to go and buy flour when we could produce it ourselves.'

So Sally found a nice little plot of land, and got it ready for sowing. Jake looked over the fence. 'Growing some wheat, are we?' he said. 'No money in wheat, these days; the big boys have got all that buttoned up. You'll never grow enough to make it pay. What do you pay for your seeds? More than you should, I'll bet. You've got to keep your unit costs in mind, you know.'

Sally smiled, and went on working. After she had got the ground ready she went into the potting shed and got her precious bag of seeds. She went out onto the plot and started scattering them around. Poor Jake nearly had a heart attack! 'You can't just go scattering seeds around like that,' he said. 'Target your resources – how often must I tell you! Look, you've gone and spilt some of them among those thistles. You'd better get them out, you know – they'll never grow there.'

'Thank you,' said Sally, and carried on sowing her seed.

Then Jake got really agitated, and shouted, 'Hey! Mind the path! Nothing will grow there, you know.'

'No, said Sally, calmly, 'I don't suppose it will.'

'Mind the rockery!' roared Jake. 'Really, Sally, I don't know how you expect ever to make a living as a farmer! Just like a woman!'

Sally decided to ignore that. She finished off her work, wished Jake a good afternoon and went inside. Jake just stood there, leaning on the fence and shaking his head in despair.

Sally looked out of the window and saw a flock of birds on the path, eating the seeds she had dropped there. 'Well', she thought, 'they've got to eat as well. And if they eat the seed on the path, they're leaving the rest alone.'

A few days later, Tom got really excited. 'Your seeds are growing,' he said to Sally. Sally looked out and, sure enough, the rockery was sprouting wheat.

'I wouldn't get too excited about that,' she said to Tom. 'There's not enough soil there, so it won't last.' Sure enough, when the sun got really hot, the wheat was scorched and it died. 'Not to worry,' said Sally. 'I expected that to happen.'

Next time Sally was outside, Jake was leaning on the fence as usual. 'I told you not to do it,' he said. 'It won't grow, you know.' Then he looked over to the thistle patch. 'There's a bit sprouting there,' he went on, 'but it won't last. You mark my words.'

He was right. It didn't last. The thistles were very strong weeds, and they'd had a lot of time to get well set in. So they just choked the new wheat shoots, and never gave them a chance.

'See,' said Jake. 'You women should really listen to us men. I don't know why your husband doesn't keep you straight.'

'What, Tom?' laughed Sally. 'Tom wouldn't know a cauliflower from a buttercup! He's a fisherman!' And she chuckled as she went inside. Tom had a good laugh when she told him, too.

Over the next few months, the plot of land started to change. Little green shots appeared first, and Sally and Tom started to get excited. Then the shoots grew tall, and very soon they were dense and high enough for rabbits and field mice to hide in them without being seen. Sally and Tom watched as the colour changed gradually, and eventually they had a wonderful plot of land filled with golden wheat waving gently in the wind.

As soon as it was ripe, Sally got Tom to act as labourer for her and they harvested the corn. Jake looked over the fence and gave them occasional advice. 'Don't miss any,' he said. 'You've got to exploit the potential of your investment to the full.'

When the wheat was gathered in, they weighed it and Sally was overjoyed. 'According to what I've worked out,' she said to Tom, 'those seeds we bought have given us thousands more in return. Some of them must have produced thirty, or sixty or even a hundred times as much!'

'Hmmph!' snorted Jake over the fence. 'If you'd been more careful, you'd have had even more.'

'If I'd followed your advice,' retorted Sally, 'I'd never have sown any seeds at all.'

Based on Matthew 13:1-9

Let's Chat

The bible says that God's foolishness
is better than our wisdom.
Can you see, now, what that means?

We're Sad

Please forgive us, God, for being so careful –
with our money, with our things,
and most of all with our love.
Teach us how much joy we can get
from throwing love around!

We're Glad

Thank you, God!
You don't take advice from 'wise' people;
you scatter love around
as though it's going out of fashion!
Thank you for giving us so much.

Let's Pray for People

Let's pray especially for lonely people.
Some people are lonely because
other people are too 'careful' with their love.
Others are lonely because they themselves
are too selfish, afraid of losing out.
Please, God, help us all to understand
that you never run out of love,
and however much we 'waste'
you will always give us more.

The Barley and the Bindweed

Sally and Jake were both farmers, and they had been friends once although they farmed in very different ways. The difference was that Jake was greedy. He always farmed every bit of his land, and never left anything behind when he harvested. He grew as much as he possibly could and he ensured that every grain of wheat, every apple and pear, every potato and cucumber was sold at the very best possible price. Every single square inch of Jake's farm was always growing something.

Sally was a lot more relaxed about things. She used to leave a bit of one of her fields wild to encourage butterflies and other beautiful wildlife. Jake thought she was mad.

'You'll never make any money out of butterflies,' he used to say. 'You have to get everything you can out of your land – that's what good farming's about.'

Sally just smiled to herself. 'Poor old Jake,' she thought. 'He'll learn the hard way.' Then she gave orders to her workers to vary the crops each year so that the fields had a change, and always to leave one field without anything growing in it. 'We've got to take care of the land,' she used to say, 'and not ask too much of it. Then it will take care of us.'

Jake thought this was just a load of sentimental nonsense. 'It's a matter of good stewardship,' he used to say. 'You've got to get all you can from the land.'

'No,' said Sally. 'Good stewardship is about caring for the land – and it'll give you more in the long run.'

'Bah! Humbug!' exclaimed Jake, and waited for Sally to go bankrupt. 'When she does, I can buy her fields at a knockdown price,' he thought. 'Then I'll show her how a *real* farmer works the land!'

Well, Jake watched and waited, and every harvest he thought he'd see Sally packing it in because it wasn't paying. But what he actually saw was Sally's farm doing better and better.

After a little while, Jake's farm started to produce smaller crops. 'I can't understand it,' his foreman said one day. 'The cabbages always used to do well in that field, but for the last year or two they've definitely been smaller.'

'Same goes for the wheat,' said Jake, sadly. 'The crop's got smaller every year for four years now. Well, we'll just have to put more seed in to make up for it.'

Sally overheard the conversation. 'If you don't mind my saying so,' she said, 'that'll just make it worse. You're taking all the goodness out of the land. Why not give it a rest for a year, and grow something different?'

'I do mind you saying so, actually,' snapped Jake. 'You go and mind your own business, Mrs. Knowitall!'

Jake was really jealous of Sally. 'She doesn't work half as hard as I do,' he complained to his foreman. 'And just look at her crops!'

Well, the years went by and Jake just could not understand what was happening. Sally's farm was thriving, with lovely rich soil producing good crops – except for whichever field it was that was resting of course – while Jake' crops got smaller and smaller. Then his soil began to go all powdery and dry, and every time there was a strong wind some of it blew away and landed on Sally's farm.

'That's the problem!' thought Jake. 'She's got better soil than I have. It's not fair. The more he thought about it, the more jealous he became – and he longed to find a way of spoiling Sally's farm. Then he had an idea. And what an idea it was!

Although he couldn't grow good food crops any more, Jake had plenty of thistles and dandelions, and enormous quantities of bindweed because they will grow anywhere, as any gardener will tell you. So he dug up some of them, and put them into his greenhouse.

When the weeds grew big, Jake very carefully saved all the seeds they produced, and then late at night, while Sally was fast asleep in bed, he put his plan into action. He went out, wearing his darkest clothes so that he wouldn't be seen, and headed for Sally's best fields. And there, among the wheat and barley crops, he scattered the thistle, dandelion a nd bindweedseeds. Then he sneaked home and waited for the crops to ripen. Every day, he would look over his hedge as Sally passed and say, 'How're the crops doing then, Sally?'

'Very nicely, thank you,' Sally used to reply, wondering why Jake was being so nice all of a sudden.

She was still wondering about this when, one morning, her foreman came running up and said, 'Quick! Come and look at the fields!' Sally hurried off to see what all the fuss was about, and there – all mixed in among the crops – were thousands of nasty looking weeds.

'I can't think what went wrong,' stammered the foreman apologetically.

'Don't worry, it's not your fault,' Sally assured him. 'This is sabotage, and I think I know who's done it.'

'Well, I'd better get them out,' said the foreman and started giving orders. 'Hey, you two! Go and get some tools, we've got weeding to do.'

'Oh no! Don't do that!' exclaimed Sally. 'You'll probably pull up some good plants as well. No, just let them grow together. My crops are strong enough to stand a bit of opposition from a few weeds. When we harvest it, that will be the time to separate them out.'

So that is exactly what they did. Sally was quite right: her crop stood up to the weeds very well, and when the harvest time came they had a grand sort out.

Jake's little plan hadn't worked at all. In fact, it was he who went out of business because he'd destroyed the very land his business depended on. Then Sally bought his farm at a bargain price and set about correcting the harm that Jake had done.

Based on Matthew 13:24-30

Let's Chat

Do we ever get jealous
when other people do well?
Do we especially resent it
if we think we deserve better?

We're Sad

Dear God, we're sorry for our jealousy.
Help us to be truly happy
when other people succeed,
and to be ready to learn from them.

We're Glad

Thank you, God, for talented people.
Thank you for people who succeed
at discovering new things,
at healing people who are sick,
at creating beautiful art.
Thank you for the pleasure they give us.

Let's Pray for People

Some people are unhappy
because they don't feel 'successful'.
But it's not compulsory to be brilliant, is it?
Please, God, help them to enjoy being truly human,
and to be proud of that.
Teach us to value people for what they are,
not for what they do,
and give us grace to show it.

The Sale of the Century

Abe was a very wealthy man. He had a big house, with lots of rooms, and each room was full of beautiful furniture. He was never cold at night, because he had lovely warm rugs on his bed and thick carpets on his floors. At every window hung colourful, heavy curtains which kept out the draughts and looked impressive as well.

Every day, Abe fed on the best food money could buy, and drank excellent wines. He really knew how to enjoy life, and he could afford to do it. His friends used to say that even if the whole world went bankrupt, Abe would be all right. He was incredibly rich.

How had he got rich? Well, Abe was a merchant. That meant that he bought and sold things – but not just any old things. Abe was a pearl trader. He used to make long journeys to visit the pearl fishers. They would spend all day diving in the sea looking for oysters which had pearls in them, and then they would sell the pearls they found to people like Abe who would take them to the markets and sell them to other people. It was a lovely business to be in, and Abe really enjoyed it.

And yet Abe was not really happy. Even with his fine house, his large stables full of beautiful horses and camels, his wonderful gardens stretching as far as the eye could see – even with all that, he was not really happy. He was sure there was a beautiful pearl out there somewhere, which he had not yet seen. Abe didn't just trade pearls for money – he actually enjoyed pearls for themselves. And he had a lifelong ambition to find his perfect pearl, but he knew that he would probably never be lucky enough to fulfil it.

Then one day, it happened.

He was walking along the beach where the pearl fishers worked when he felt a nudge and heard a voice say. 'Want to see something really special?'

There was something familiar about the voice, which made Abe turn and look. It was Josh, one of the pearl fishers.

'It's a pearl!' he said. 'That pearl you've always been after.'

'Look, Josh, I don't mind a joke,' said Abe, 'but it's been a really hard day, so just drop it will you?'

'No wind-up, Guv – honest!' said Josh. 'Go on – won't hurt to look. What've you got to lose?'

'All right, Josh,' said Abe, wearily, 'but it'd better not be a wind-up. Let's have a look, then.'

Josh looked horrified. 'What, here? D'you want the whole world to know about it? Lord love me, Guv, I couldn't sleep safe in me bed if I thought anyone knew.' With that, Josh led Abe to a deserted corner of the beach, and then, looking furtively around him, drew back some branches from the mouth of a cave. 'No one knows about this, Guv,' he said. 'Get in, quick.'

Once inside, Josh lit a candle and rummaged under a pile of moss. Then, before Abe's amazed eyes, he brought out the most wonderful pearl Abe had ever seen. More than that, it was beyond anything he could ever have imagined. It was

perfectly round, with a silky smooth surface, and seemed to absorb the light of the candle. In return, it gave off all the colours of the rainbow. Abe just stood there, absolutely entranced by it. And in that moment he knew that this was the chance to fulfil his life's ambition.

As Abe turned to face Josh, he did his best to look casual. 'It's, er, quite a nice one,' he said. 'How much d'you want for it?'

Josh was now full of confidence. He'd known that all he had to do was to get Abe to look at it and it would be sold. 'Come off it, Guvn'r,' he said. 'It's not "quite nice" – it's absolutely stupendous. You've never seen anything like it before and I doubt you will again. Now if you want it it's yours, but if you don't I can soon find another punter.'

'Oh, no! Don't do that!' gasped Abe. 'How much d'you want for it?'

'Well,' said Josh. 'I'm not a greedy man. All I want is a big house, a stable full of fine horses, and enough money to keep me in luxury the rest of my life. Shall we say a million?'

Abe nearly died of heart failure. That would take everything he'd got. His nice house, his stables, his fine clothes and furniture – everything he'd worked for all his life would have to be sold to buy this one pearl.

'I don't know,' he said. 'That's an awful lot of money.'

'It's an awful lot of pearl,' said Josh. 'Still, if you don't want it . . .'

'Hold on – I never said that!' said Abe, hastily. 'All right. I'll get the money.'

Abe sold his house, with all its furniture and equipment, and went to live in a tent. He sold his horses and camels, and all the other things he had. Then he went to the bank and drew out all his money, and eventually he just managed to scrape together the million that Josh wanted. Then he went back to see Josh. 'There you are,' he said. 'You can count it if you like.'

'I will,' said Josh, and when he had, he handed over the pearl to Abe. 'Tell me, Guv,' he said, 'what makes you want this so badly that you've sold everything you worked for just to buy this one pearl?'

'Well,' said Abe. 'Some things are worth much more than money, or comfort. You have to be prepared to give up the less important things if you want to have what's really valuable.'

Based on Matthew 13:45-46

Let's Chat

For some people, it's pearls,
for others it's cars or computers.
What about things like love,
truth, friendship, community?

We're Sad

Please forgive us, God,
for clinging to things
which can't make us happy,
and ignoring the things that can.
Help us to treasure love and goodness,
and each other.

We're Glad

Thank you, God, for giving us your love.
Thank you for showing us
just how important we are
by sacrificing everything for us.
Teach us to love and value one another
the way you love and value us.

Let's Pray for People

We pray for people who miss out
on the really wonderful things of life,
because they're trying to cling on
to things that aren't as good.
Please, God, help all people
to treasure the things that are important to you.

Peter Gets His Feet Wet

After Jesus had fed the five thousand people, he and his disciples were very tired. 'I think it's time we got away,' said Jesus. 'Peter looks about done in.'

'Who? Me?' said Peter, rubbing his eyes and trying not to yawn. 'I'm not tired.'

'Really?' laughed Jesus. 'Well, if we pass any sheep on the way home, just don't count them, that's all.'

Philip joined in the conversation. 'I don't know what makes you think you're going to get away,' he said. 'This crowd's determined to make you king, and they're not about to be fobbed off.'

'I think you're right,' said Jesus. 'I'll tell you what. You all go home, and I'll follow you later. It's me they want, so as long as I'm here they won't follow you, and then I can slip away quietly.'

'You're not thinking, Jesus,' said Peter. 'If we've taken the boat, how are you going to get across the lake?'

'I imagine I'll think of something,' Jesus replied, 'but if you all hang around with me none of us will get away.'

'He's right, you know,' said Thomas. 'Look, I vote we do as he says. He's a pretty resourceful chap and we ought to trust him more.'

So while Jesus carried on holding the crowd's attention, the disciples slipped quietly away and put out to sea expecting Jesus to follow them very soon and signal them to pick him up. But Jesus didn't do that. Instead, he persuaded the crowd to go home and then went off to a quiet place on his own to pray. He had had people around him all day long and even Jesus sometimes found it difficult to listen to God properly in a crowd.

Meanwhile, the disciples were getting worried. They were quite a distance from the shore, and the sky was looking threatening.

'Let's go back and find him,' suggested Matthew.

'He won't like that one little bit,' said James. 'You know he hates being fussed over, and he always seems to get by. He's really an amazing fellow.'

'Well,' said John, 'we've got to do one or the other. We either go back or we go home, but if we stay here we're going to be caught in that storm that's brewing up.'

'That's it,' said Andrew, whose boat it was. 'We're going home. That's what Jesus told us to do, and anyway he's probably found somewhere to shelter for the night. We can come back for him in the morning, after the storm's over. Peter, get that sail up and let's get moving before it's too late.'

Up went the sail, and before long the boat was cutting through the water towards Galilee.

Just as they thought they were going to make it, the wind changed and the water around the boat started thrashing violently. For hours and hours, they battled to keep the ship afloat, but it seemed to be useless. Then, in the early hours of the morning, Andrew saw something that really made his hair stand on end. He nudged James and said, 'L-l-look over there.' When James looked he forgot about the storm and just stood staring with his mouth wide open.

'Hey, you two!' bellowed Peter. 'Don't just stand there and leave all the work to us.'

James and Andrew didn't answer. They were so amazed and so frightened that they couldn't speak a word. James just raised his hand and pointed a very shaky finger indeed back towards the shore they had come from. Peter looked where James was pointing and what do you think he saw? He saw a man – not standing on the shore but walking towards them on the top of the water. He couldn't believe his eyes. Not only was it impossible then; it's still impossible even now!

After a few moments Andrew found his voice. 'It's a ghost!' he said. 'And it's after us.'

Then the 'ghost' called out to them. 'Don't be afraid. It's me – Jesus.'

'Oh, my life! It speaks as well!' wailed Andrew, who hadn't listened properly to what Jesus said.

Peter had heard clearly, though. 'Is that really you?' he called out. 'If it is, can I come and meet you?'

'Of course you can,' answered Jesus. 'Just keep your eyes on me and you'll be all right.'

Now, anyone else would have stepped out very carefully onto that raging sea – if they'd done it at all – but not Peter. He just climbed up on the side of the boat and jumped. And sure enough, he stayed on the top, just like Jesus. He could hardly believe it was happening. He took a few steps toward Jesus, and found that he could keep his balance quite easily although the sea was still pounding up and down. Then he got a bit silly.

'Hey, fellas! Look at me!' he called, turning round to look at his friends in the boat, 'It's easy! It's a piece of cake! It's Ahh! Oh!! HEEEEEELP!'

Peter had gone right under the water. All his friends were very frightened, but Jesus just hurried over, reached out his hand and pulled Peter back to the surface again. 'Why won't you ever listen to me, and do as I say!' he exclaimed. 'I told you to keep looking at me – not start showing off to your friends. Come on, let's get you into the boat.'

As soon as they got into the boat, the storm stopped. Just like that! The sea was calm again and they could go on their way.

It was then that the disciples realised that Jesus was no ordinary man, and they worshipped him. And not only they but all the people around started to recognise him and brought sick people to be healed by him.

As for Peter, he said he'd learnt his lesson. 'From now on', he said, 'I'll always keep my eyes on him in a crisis. I'll always trust him, and stick with him.'

He meant it, too. He found out later that it wasn't that easy, and he let Jesus down rather badly a few times, but he came through in the end. He found that keeping his eye on Jesus didn't always make life easy for him – but it certainly made it interesting!

Based on Matthew 14:22-33

Let's Chat

Does life sometimes seem like a great, chaotic sea?
Do we find it difficult to keep on top of things?
Even though we don't walk on water,
a little faith can still go a long way!

We're Sad

Sometimes, Jesus, life gets so busy
that we forget about you.
We're sorry.
Help us to trust you,
and to keep our eyes on you.

We're Glad

Wonderful God,
thank you for being there for us,
especially when we feel out of our depth.

Let's Pray for People

We pray for people who get swamped by life,
who always have too much to do
and not enough time or energy to get through.
Help us to be 'Jesus' for them:
to hold out a hand to help,
and to show them that you care for them.

Jesus Gets Angry

Dan, the money changer was setting up his stall as usual in the temple. Next to him, in his accustomed place, was Joe, a dove merchant. Now all this might seem very strange to you, but there was a simple reason for it. It was rather like what happens in this country, when people visit friends in hospital and find flower sellers there. It's just convenient to be able to buy the things you need when you get there. In the same way, people who went to the temple needed doves because they were used in the worship, so it made sense for them to be sold there. And they needed special money, as well, to put in the offering, so Dan was there to change their ordinary money into special temple money. That all seems perfectly reasonable, but you know the old saying, 'It ain't what you do, it's the way that you do it'.

'I like it here,' Dan was saying. 'Better than standing outside in the rain.'

'Yes, said Joe. 'Mind you, I sometimes get a bit embarrassed about the space we take up. It makes it difficult for less able people to get in when these stalls are all over the place.'

'Who cares about them?' scoffed Dan. 'They've never got any money anyway.'

'That's true,' said Joe, 'and of course there's another advantage to being in here.'

'What's that?' asked Dan.

'Simple,' said Joe. 'It's harder for the customers to compare our prices with the ordinary shops. And once they're in they don't feel like going back out anyway, so we can charge extra.'

'That's true,' said Dan. 'It's a pretty good swindle – and it's legal!' And they both laughed.

'Just a minute,' said Joe. 'What's all that noise outside?'

They listened carefully. There seemed to be some kind of celebration going on. They could just about make out words like 'Hosanna!' but they couldn't understand what it was about. Then a man they thought they'd seen before strode into the temple with some others just behind him, and stood looking around with a disapproving expression on his face.

'Isn't that that Jesus character?' asked Joe. 'He doesn't look very happy – d'you think he's going to cause trouble?'

'What! Him?' laughed Dan. 'He's a wimp! Talks about "love" and "forgiveness" all the time. Do you know, he actually tells people that if someone hits them they should let them do it again?'

'No!' exclaimed Joe, and they roared with laughter.

Jesus carried on looking round for a few moments, and seemed to get more and more angry. Then he turned to Andrew who was near to him. 'Look at this!' he said. 'There are all these sick and disabled people outside who can't get in here, and all the space is taken up by these money-grabbing swindlers!'

Andrew was worried. He knew Jesus a little better than Dan and Joe did! 'Why don't we just go and find a quiet drink somewhere?' he asked. 'It's been a big day for you.'

Jesus didn't hear him. He was too concerned with what was happening. Suddenly, he grabbed a piece of rope which one of the traders had left lying around, and knotted it to make a vicious looking whip. He went over to Joe.

'What do you people think you're doing?' he asked, in a voice that was just a little too quiet and controlled.

'Just a bit of honest trade, sir,' grinned Joe. 'Can I interest you in a pair of doves? Best prices in town.'

'Best prices for *you*, you mean,' said Jesus. And then, without warning, he grabbed the front of Joe's stall and turned it over. The cages burst open and doves started flying everywhere while Joe frantically ran to and fro trying to catch them. Then Jesus went over to Dan.

'Now look here,' Dan said hastily, 'I've got a licence to trade here; I paid a high bribe – I mean tax – for it.' But Jesus wasn't listening. He grabbed Dan's tray of money and threw it on the floor, and then picked up his table and turned it upside down. Well, there was pandemonium. All those holy people suddenly got very interested in what was rolling around the floor. Worshippers were scrabbling around in the dust and fighting over the most valuable coins. Then Jesus went over to the animal pens and drove the animals out of the temple. The owners went after them to try to catch them, and Joe and Dan also decided to cut their losses and leave at the same time. The scramble for money died down as the best coins were snapped up, and by the time the temple police arrived it was all over. Well, nothing changes, does it!

Then a wonderful thing happened. Into the temple came a procession of people who had never been in there before. Some of them couldn't walk and had to be carried by others on stretchers; others could only walk with help from somebody else; yet others were blind and had to have someone to guide them. They came over to where Jesus was standing, still a little out of breath, and the first one, who was leaning on a stick, spoke to him.

'Thank you,' he said. 'We haven't been able to get in before. The traders took up so much room, and all the people bustling about doing their shopping meant that only the really fit people could cope with it.'

'I know,' said Jesus, 'and it makes me angry! People should

be a lot more considerate, but while you're here why don't we do something about that leg of yours?'

'No good,' said the man. 'I've tried every doctor in the area, but it's incurable.'

Jesus took hold of his hand and lifted his weight off the stick, and suddenly the man's leg grew strong again. While he was standing there on both feet, looking amazed, Jesus moved on to the next person. Soon the temple was full of people laughing, singing and praising God while they jumped and ran around celebrating their new found health and strength.

From then on, a lot of new people joined in things at the temple, who had never been able to get in before. They were very happy about it, although Dan and Joe and their friends weren't. But then, you can't please everybody, can you? So why try?

Based on Matthew 21:12-14

Let's Chat

Does it seem strange
to think of Jesus being angry?

We're Sad

We say patience is a virtue,
but sometimes that's an excuse.
We're sorry, God, for being too tolerant
when other people are getting hurt.
Help us to know when it's right to be patient,
and when we should protest.

We're Glad

Thank you, loving God,
for people who protest against evil.
Thank you for using them
to make the world a better place for us all.

Let's Pray for People

We pray for people who are kept out,
who aren't able to protest for themselves
and get brushed aside.
Especially we pray for disabled people
in a world run by the able bodied.
Please, God, help us to be angry for them,
and give us the courage to protest.

'Are You a Friend of Jesus?'

Peter was a friend of Jesus. In fact he was a very special friend. He was one of the twelve who were very close to Jesus; the ones whom Jesus was preparing to carry on his work after he went away. And Peter was going to be their leader when that happened. So he must have been a very special person mustn't he?

Peter knew he would never let Jesus down. He told him so, as well. Whenever he got the chance, he said to Jesus, 'I'll always be your friend. Whatever happens, and however tough it gets, I'll be with you.'

He meant it – every word. And he meant it when he said, 'Even if I have to die for you, I won't ever let you down.' Peter really loved Jesus – and he simply couldn't imagine that he might ever do or say anything to hurt him. After all, Peter was a brave man. He often had to go out fishing at night on rough seas, and of course he was sometimes frightened – who wouldn't be with the wind strong enough to blow away a mountain and the waves as high as houses? But he'd never gone to pieces, and he'd always kept his nerve and done his job. So he thought that he would always be rock solid in a crisis.

In fact, Jesus had said that, hadn't he? Peter used to be called Simon, but Jesus changed it. 'I'm going to call you Peter,' he said. 'You're a rock – and it's on this rock that I will build my church.' So Peter had every reason to be confident.

One evening, Jesus arranged to celebrate a special meal with his disciples, and afterwards he suggested going out for a walk. As they were walking, Peter heard Jesus say something very strange. 'You're all going to break down,' he said. 'You're all going to run away and leave me when things go wrong.'

Peter was horrified. 'Not us, Jesus!' he said. 'We're never going to let you down. And even if the rest of them do, I won't – I'll be right with you, even if I have to die.'

Jesus looked at him, and Peter saw that his eyes were full of love but also full of pain. 'Peter,' he said, 'I know you mean well, but by the time the cock crows in the morning you'll have said you don't even know me – three times.'

'Who Me?!' replied the astonished Peter. 'Never! I'm no chicken – I'll stick with you even if all of that lot don't.'

'Hey!' said Matthew. 'Who're you calling "that lot"? We'll all stick together, whatever happens, won't we lads?'

'Oh yes,' they all said. 'We won't let Jesus down.'

'Well, just stay here, all of you,' said Jesus. 'I'm going over there to pray.'

It was very late at night, and the disciples were very tired. They didn't mean to fall asleep, but fall asleep they did, until the noise woke them up.

'There he is! After him! Don't let him get away!'

There seemed to be soldiers everywhere. The whole place was full of noise, and the light of torches, and there seemed to be a riot going on. Peter looked around, expecting to see Jesus running for his life, but Jesus was standing calmly waiting for the guards to get to him. Peter grabbed a sword and rushed forward. He swung the sword high in the air and brought it down on one of the men, narrowly missing his head and slicing off his ear. Before anybody could do anything, Jesus stepped forward in front of Peter, and said, 'No, that's not right. Let me deal with this my own way.' Then he reached out and healed the man's ear.

Peter couldn't believe it! What was Jesus playing at? All that stuff about loving your enemies was fine in theory, but Jesus should have know it was no way to handle this! Then Peter looked around and saw more guards streaming towards them. If they didn't move fast they'd be surrounded. 'Take cover, everybody!' he yelled and dived into the bushes, closely followed by all Jesus' other friends.

When they had got away, they realised that Jesus wasn't with them, and looked round just in time to see him being tied up and taken away. 'Come on,' said James. 'There's nothing we can do here.' But Peter couldn't bring himself just to leave Jesus. As the others ran away, he crouched low in the shadows, and followed to see where the guards took Jesus. Soon he found himself at the High Priest's house, where Jesus was put on trial. Peter sneaked in – it was a cold night for standing outside – and warmed his hands by a fire in the courtyard while he listened to what was going on inside. People were telling dreadful lies about Jesus, and trying to find excuses to kill him. Peter couldn't think what to do, and then one of the servants spotted him.

'Hey you!' she said. 'You're one of his friends, aren't you!'

'Who? Me?' blurted Peter in panic. 'I don't know what you're talking about.'

'Yes you are,' said someone else. 'I've seen you with him.'

'Not me!' said Peter. 'Never seen him before in my life!'

Then a third person said, 'I know you're one of his mob – you've got a northern accent. You're all the same you northerners – a bunch of dangerous revolutionaries.'

Peter was in a real stew by now, and he wasn't thinking before he spoke. 'Honestly,' he said, 'as God's my judge, I don't know him.'

It was then that Peter heard a terrible sound. Have you any idea what it was?

It was the cock crowing. The most dreadful sound that he had ever heard in his entire life, because he remembered what Jesus had said.

He'd really done it now! Peter, the rock, the strong one, the solid, faithful friend who would never let Jesus down! But Jesus had been right all along.

Peter felt terrible. He could feel the tears coming into his eyes, and he pushed his way through the crowd to get outside. As soon as he was out of sight of everybody, he collapsed in a heap on the ground and cried and cried and cried!

Peter learnt a lot from that. He learnt that he wasn't as strong as he thought. He learnt that it's best not to make rash promises unless you're quite sure you can keep them. And a little while later, he learnt something really wonderful. He learnt that even when people let Jesus down as badly as that, they can still be forgiven and still be Jesus' friend.

Peter went on to be a very important disciple, just as Jesus had promised he would. But that's another story, for another time.

Based on Matthew 26:30-38, 51-60, 69-75

Let's Chat

It isn't always easy to be a friend.
Can you think of times when you've been tempted
to let a friend down?

We're Sad

We're sorry we're not always brave, Jesus.
We like being friends, but sometimes
it just seems too hard.
Forgive us for any times
when we've let people down,
and let you down at the same time.
Please help us to do better.

We're Glad

Thank you, God, for all our friends.
Thank you especially for the really good ones
who forgive us if we get things wrong.
Thank you for showing your love
through our family and friends.

Let's Pray for People

We pray for people who feel alone
because they haven't got any friends,
or because they've been let down in the past.
And we pray for people who feel guilty
about letting their friends down.
Please, God, give us all the chance
to start again.

THE VOICE IN THE WILDERNESS

There was once a priest called Zechariah, who was married to Elizabeth. For a long time they had not been able to have a family, but then, just as they thought they were too old, they had a son, John. Elizabeth and Zechariah thought he was a real blessing from God – but there were times when they could have found other words for him! The problem was that John used to embarrass them because he never combed his hair and he always went around in old, scruffy clothes. If his parents bought him new ones, he just refused to wear them.

One day, Elizabeth shouted at John, 'I'm fed up with you going around looking as though you don't belong to anybody. Why don't you tidy yourself up!'

'There are more important things than looking good, Mother,' answered John – and found his pocket money stopped for a week for being cheeky. But that did not seem to worry him very much, either. 'There are more important things than money, as well,' he said, and got sent to bed without his supper.

Now his parents were very good people, and they loved John more than they could say, but it's just the way it is – even the nicest children embarrass their parents occasionally . . . and religious people are especially easy to embarrass.

'What will the neighbours say?' moaned Elizabeth, one day.

'Never mind the neighbours!' answered Zechariah. 'What will the *congregation* say?'

When John grew up, he didn't get any tidier, or any more careful about money. He seemed to Zechariah to be developing some very strange ideas. Worse still, he'd got some friends who thought the same, and they used to go off together for weeks on end, camping in the desert and washing themselves all the time. They said that was a sign of being made clean, because they always seemed to feel guilty.

Then John started preaching, and his father cringed with embarrassment. 'Repent your sins!' John shouted. 'Prepare to meet your God!'

The trouble was, lots of people seemed to believe John when he said that God's judgment was coming, and he spent weeks at a time at the river Jordan baptising people. One day, some of Zechariah's friends, who were also priests, offered to help. 'We'll talk to him,' they said. 'He'll listen to us.' So they put on their best robes and went to see John.

When he saw them coming, John pointed at them and shouted at the top of his voice, 'Ooh, you wicked people! You snakes! Don't come to me for easy forgiveness! You just wait until you see what God is going to do to you. You think you're so special, but you're not. God could make better priests than you out of stones!'

Well, the priests were terribly embarrassed. After all, no one minds if ordinary people do a few things they shouldn't, but everyone gets terribly upset if a priest does anything wrong – no matter how tiny. So the priests had to pretend to be especially good, even though they knew they weren't. And John wasn't helping their public image one little bit!

One of them, whose name was Levi, went up to John. 'Just who do you think you are? Elijah or somebody?' he asked. 'Perhaps you think you're a great prophet come back to life.'

'All I am,' said John, 'is a voice – a voice in the wilderness warning you of someone greater who is following me. Someone so great that I'm not good enough even to help him take off his shoes.'

Levi didn't get the chance to answer, because John was suddenly surrounded by people wanting to know what to do to stop God being angry with them. 'Share everything you have,' he said, 'and treat poor people fairly.'

'What about me?' asked Matthew, the tax collector.

'Charge people a fair tax,' said John, 'and don't fiddle the books.' Everybody laughed at that, because they hated tax collectors.

'What should *we* do?' asked some soldiers.

'Don't abuse your power,' John answered, 'and be satisfied with your pay.'

'And what about me?' asked a quiet voice. 'Will you baptise me?'

John stopped and stared in amazement. It was Jesus, the local carpenter. 'I can't baptise you,' John protested. 'You're good – it's you who should baptise me.'

Levi and his friends were horrified! How could John call this common carpenter good, after all he'd said about them? But while they were watching, Jesus went into the water with John to be baptised. As they came up out of the water, an amazing thing happened. It looked as though a dove was hovering over Jesus – but everyone knows that doves can't hover. That was the first strange thing, but it got stranger. There was a voice – an interesting kind of voice, not quite like anything the people had heard before. Was it a man? Was it a woman? Was it a child? It wasn't shouting, and yet it could be clearly heard.

'This is my son, whom I love very much,' said the voice. So of course Levi thought it must be Joseph, but he couldn't see him anywhere. When Levi looked back, he was surprised because the dove had gone and everything seemed normal. Jesus was drying himself off on a towel, and John was talking to him.

Levi was puzzled. Had he imagined it all? He'd have liked to think that, but his friends seemed to have seen it as well. 'It must have been real,' said one of them. 'We heard it with our own ears.'

Oh, that doesn't mean anything,' said Levi, 'I'm sure there's a natural explanation. After all, we're educated men, and we know better than to trust our experience.'

Even so, Levi couldn't help being a little worried as he and his friends went away to see Zechariah and Elizabeth.

'Well,' said Zechariah, 'what happened? Did he listen to you?

'Had he combed his hair recently?' asked Elizabeth.

'I'm afraid it's bad news,' said Levi. 'He's obviously not going to listen to us, and he's got some really strange friends. I don't think we've heard the last of them by a long way.'

Based on Mark 1:1-11

Let's Chat

What a strange person John the Baptist was!
Being different isn't necessarily bad.

We're Sad

Sometimes we make fun of people
or refuse to take them seriously,
just because they are different.
Please, God, forgive us if we've been hurtful,
or if we've missed something important
that you were trying to tell us.

We're Glad

It's good that we're not all the same;
what a dull world it would be!
Thank you, God, for people
who challenge us, and make us think.
Thank you for speaking to us
even when we're too proud to listen!

Let's Pray for People

Please, God, help us to listen to you
when you speak through people
who seem to us to be strange.
Help both us and them
to realise how important they are.

Perfectly Willing to Learn

Lydia was rather an angry woman. She tended to rub people up the wrong way by being aggressive, and that meant that she hadn't got many friends. It was a shame, because she was a very nice person; she was just angry about always being treated differently from other people because she came from another country. One of her neighbours, a man called Andy, tried to help her by giving her a little advice.

'You should try to be more like us,' he said. 'After all, "When in Rome, do as the Romans do".'

'You hypocrite!' Lydia said. 'To begin with, you hate the Romans, and for another thing, when you go abroad you behave just the same as you do at home – so why shouldn't I?'

'I'm sorry,' said Andy. 'Please don't misunderstand. I'm not prejudiced, you know. Some of my best friends are foreigners. I just think it would be better if you were all like us.'

'I think you'd better go, before I'm rude to you,' said Lydia.

It really did seem terribly unfair. Lydia was from Syria, as were quite a number of people in her district. They all lived in the same area because they felt safer that way. If they went to live anywhere else people were rude to them, and got up petitions about them because they thought their houses might be worth less money if 'Syroes' lived in the neighbourhood. So they all lived close together in their own communities, and were accused of being unfriendly and not mixing! They couldn't win. Then, of course, if they tried to live like everyone else they were told that they were pretending to be something they weren't, and if they lived in their own way, someone would come along and say, 'When in Rome, do as the Romans do.' It really was a no-win situation, and you can understand why Lydia was angry – just like a lot of her friends.

Lydia had a daughter, whose name was Ria. Ria was a lovely little girl, just nine years of age, but she was very unhappy. She got teased in the street, and called a 'Syro brat', and when she tried to play with other children they bullied her. Then if she didn't try to play with them they called her a 'stuck up little

Syro' and shouted nasty things like, 'Syroes go home!' after her. Gradually, she got more and more unhappy, and wouldn't go out to play. Then she started locking herself away in her room and crying, and nothing anyone could do or say seemed to help. Next, she started shouting at her parents and blaming them for living in a foreign country, but it was when she started sneaking out to throw stones at local people that Lydia decided she really had to do something. She didn't mind Ria being angry – she was right to be angry – but she certainly needed to be helped to handle it.

One day, she heard that the famous healer, Jesus, was in the area. Now of course, Ria wasn't actually sick – it was the horrible people around them that were sick – but Lydia knew that Ria certainly needed a kind of healing, if she was not to be destroyed by her own anger. So she decided to go and see Jesus and ask him to help.

Meanwhile, Jesus had gone for a break. He was very tired and needed time to rest, think and pray. His friends were even more tired than he was. So they found a house to stay in for a few days, and thought they would have a bit of a holiday.

Just as they were walking down the road towards the house, and dreaming of a nice drink, a hot bath and a long snooze, they heard a sound that made their blood run cold!

'Excuse me! Jesus! Over here! Sorry to be a nuisance, but . . .'

'If you're sorry, why are you doing it?' snapped Peter. 'We've had a terrible few days.'

'That's right,' said James. 'Go away and come back next week – or preferably next year.'

Lydia wasn't going to be put off half so easily as that. She had always had to fight for her place in the world, and she was quite capable of taking on a dozen or so men!

'I'm talking to the organ grinder,' she said. 'Not his pet monkey.'

That shut Peter up – he'd never even heard of an organ grinder!

'You can't talk to us like that,' said James. 'We're his special friends, you know. He's going to make us important people in his kingdom – our mum's arranging it, isn't she, John?'*

* see Matthew 20:20-23

'Yes,' said John, 'so you just watch your manners.'

By now, Jesus had decided that he'd better do something. If the noise went on, everybody in the town would know he was there. 'What's going on?' he asked.

'Oh, nothing important, Jesus,' said John. 'It's just this Syro woman who's making a commotion. Tell her to go away.'

Jesus looked at the woman and asked, 'What do you want?'

'I just want my daughter healed,' she said. 'She's full of all kinds of anger and resentment – not that I blame her for that – but it's beginning to get to her and she's started to do terrible things. Can you help?'

'I don't know,' said Jesus. 'I've got to provide for the people of Israel first. It's not right to take food from the children and feed it to the dogs.'

Lydia was amazed! She had never expected to hear that from Jesus – not from what she had heard about him. He was famous for his gentleness, his openness and his enormous love for people. Could she have heard him correctly? Now if it had been anyone else, they would probably have got the rough end of Lydia's tongue for saying something like that, but she was still hoping Jesus would help Ria. So she took a few deep breaths, counted to ten and tried again.

'Even the dogs get the scraps that fall from the table,' she said.

Jesus looked at her, and his face and his voice grew kinder. 'You're a shrewd one!' he said. 'All right – I'm sorry. You've persuaded me. Go on home, and you'll find your daughter in a much better frame of mind.'

He was as good as his word. When Lydia went home, Ria was a lot calmer, and she and Lydia found other ways of dealing with silly prejudiced people.

James couldn't get over the way Jesus had spoken. 'You let her change your mind, Jesus,' he said. 'Surely you're not admitting you were wrong – especially to a *foreigner.'*

'There's nothing to be ashamed of in making the odd mistake,' said Jesus. 'Only in being too pig headed to admit it. I'm perfectly willing to learn.'

Then the disciples knew that Jesus really was a most extraordinary person.

Based on Mark 7:24-30

Let's Chat

Even Jesus was willing to learn;
what about us?

We're Sad

It's nice to think we know everything,
but we don't of course.
Please, God, forgive our pride
and make us more like Jesus;
willing to learn from others,
including people who seem to need our help.

We're Glad

Thank you, God,
for all the variety of people in the world.
Thank you for the things we can learn
from people of different cultures
who have experiences and knowledge,
a well as ideas to share with us.
Thank you for sending them to open our eyes.

Let's Pray for People

We're glad there are so many different kinds
of people in the world!
Please, God, help people who are frightened,
who find differences threatening.
Help us all to live together
in this wonderful kaleidoscope world
which you have made.

SPEECHLESS WITH SURPRISE

Zechariah couldn't believe what was happening to him! It had started just like any ordinary Sabbath day, with him going to lead worship. It was a very special honour, and only priests could do it. He had to go right into the 'holy of holies' as it was known, behind a curtain. No one could go there unless he was a priest – I say 'he' because only men could become priests, then. And you couldn't just decide to become a priest, either – you had to be born into the 'right' family! So Zechariah was very proud of the special job he did, and always tried to do it as well as possible.

This particular morning, though, he was a little bit distracted. You see, he and his wife, Elizabeth, were very unhappy because they didn't have any children. And they were even more unhappy because everybody seemed to think it was Elizabeth's fault. She must have upset God in some way, they thought, so that he had made her 'barren'. It simply never seemed to occur to them that it might be her husband who had the problem! Anyway, that was on Zechariah's mind a bit, as he began the ceremony in the holy of holies.

As he began to light the incense, Zechariah realised that he wasn't alone in the sanctuary – and he should have been! Out of the corner of his eye, he could see a figure standing by his shoulder. 'Whoever you are, you'd better go,' he said. 'You know only the duty priest is allowed in here.' Still the figure didn't move. 'Look, said Zechariah,' if you've got a problem, you can make an appointment to come and see me – but it won't be until the week after next, mind you, and even then it'll only be an hour because I've got a lot of forms to fill in for the High Priest. Now I'd go if I were you before God strikes you dead or something.'

'Oh, I don't think he'll do that,' said the visitor. 'He doesn't often strike angels dead, you know. We've had the odd one that's fallen from grace, but that's quite another story.'

Zechariah was startled. He looked around, and sure enough the Archangel Gabriel himself was there.

'Well, knock me down with a feather!' said Zechariah.

'Not right now,' said Gabriel. 'I want a word with you. It's just to say that God's going to give you and Elizabeth a son. You're to call him John, and he'll be a really great man – he's going to prepare the way for the Messiah you've all been waiting for.'

'Is that what you've come here for?' asked the indignant Zechariah. 'Have you come just to tease an old man? Look, my wife's old. So am I, of course, but we men don't show it as much, do we? Anyway, we're too old to have children and that's it. And if we did have a child, he wouldn't be called John, anyway. There've been Zechariah's in my family for generations, and no one has ever had a common old name like John!'

'Have you finished? asked Gabriel. 'I hope you have, because that's the last word you're going to say for a bit. This is me you're talking to – Gabriel – Supreme Archangel, and trusted ambassador of God himself. I've taken more messages for God than your entire family's had hot dinners, and no one , *no one,* I tell you, has ever called me a liar before. No, it's no good trying to protest, because you can't talk – so for once you're going to have to listen. It's time you priests learned to do that anyway. As I said, you're going to have a son. You'll call him John, and he'll be a great preacher who will prepare the way for the Messiah. Got it? Oh, sorry, you can't speak can you? Well, that will give your congregation a bit of a break. Toodle-oo!'

Suddenly, Zechariah was alone again. The archangel had gone, and, just as he had said, Zechariah was completely unable to speak. Outside, the congregation were getting impatient because he should have started the service, and Zechariah had to try to signal to them that he'd lost his voice.

'He must have seen a vision,' said one of the worshippers.

'Rubbish!' said another. 'It's that incense that's got to him. I've said it before and I'll say it again, worship should be plain and simple without all that "high synagogue" nonsense.'

Elizabeth had two shocks when Zechariah went home: to begin with he couldn't speak, and then he wrote her a note saying she was going to have a baby. She was overjoyed, and even more so when she found that her cousin Mary was pregnant as well.

By the time the baby was born, the whole neighbourhood was excited. Everyone was talking about it – well, everyone except Zechariah. And when the baby was born the neighbours came round and they all sang hymns to celebrate – well, all except Zechariah. Then one of the neighbours asked, 'What are you going to call him?'

'We're going to call him John,' Elizabeth answered.

They were all amazed. 'Why John?' they asked. 'You're supposed to call him after one of Zechariah's family. You can't call him John!'

Zechariah got a bit cross with the neighbours for laughing about it, and grabbed a piece of parchment and a pen. He wrote down, 'His name's John, and that's an end to it.'

'All right,' said Sam, his next door neighbour, 'no need to be stroppy.'

'I'm not being stroppy!' roared Zechariah. 'Hey, I can talk!'

Everyone laughed, and the celebrations began again. They went on well into the night, and this time Zechariah could join in properly.

Based on Luke 1:5-25

Let's Chat

How many mouths have you got?
And how many ears?
Do you listen twice as much as you talk?

We're Sad

We're sorry, God, for not listening.
Sometimes we're so full of our own ideas
that we don't pay attention.
Then we don't hear what you want to say.

We're Glad

Thank you, loving God,
for speaking to us in lots of different ways.
Thank you, also, for people who listen well.
They show how much they care,
and how much you love us.

Let's Pray for People

There are people who can't hear at all,
and some of them can't speak.
Please, God, help them to take part
in the world we share.
Teach us how to communicate,
and help us make the world
more friendly towards them.

The Women's Story

This is the story of Mary. She lived a very long time ago in a town called Nazareth. Yes, that's right – *that* Mary. She wasn't very old – perhaps sixteen or thereabouts – but in those days girls got married very young, and people were beginning to talk. 'What about Mary?' they used to say. 'She's on the shelf you know – should be married and have a family by now.'

Sometimes, people used to say even nastier things like, 'After all, having babies is what women are for, isn't it? And if she can't get a husband there's no way she can do that.' The trouble was that even people who didn't say that kind of thing sometimes still thought it, deep down. Where Mary came from, women weren't thought to be very important – and if they hadn't got a husband then they weren't important at all. But God was about to change all of that, as we shall see later.

Mary used to get upset, sometimes, about the cruel things people said about her, but the person she was really sorry for was her cousin Elizabeth. Elizabeth was much older than Mary, and married, and yet she didn't have any children. If Mary ever asked about that, Elizabeth just used to say, 'If I were going to have any children, it would have happened by now. No, I expect you'll be a mother before I am, at this rate.'

So of course, when people weren't gossiping about Mary they were being unkind to Elizabeth. 'Not much of a wife, is she?' they used to say. 'Can't even give her husband a baby.'

Mary was very sad about that, and every time she prayed she asked God to help her cousin Elizabeth to have a baby.

One day, Mary was doing some work around the house. There was a broken chair and she knew that if she waited for her father to mend it then it would never be done, so she went and found some tools and some glue and settled down to work. Just as she got to a very tricky part of the job, she heard a voice say, 'Hello, Mary.'

'That's strange,' thought Mary. 'I'm not expecting any visitors.' She didn't want to look up in case she let her hand slip and ruined her work, so she just kept her head down and carried on. 'It must have been the wind,' she thought to herself.

Then the voice came again: 'Mary.'

This time Mary knew it must be real, but she didn't want to lose track of her work. So she kept her head down and her eye on what she was doing, and said, 'Hello. Who's that?'

'I'm the Archangel Gabriel,' said the voice.

Mary was just about to say, 'Yes, and I'm the queen of Sheba,' when something made her look up – and there he was! Mary was speechless at first. I mean, what do you say to an angel? Normally, she would have offered any visitor a seat and some food and drink, but she didn't know whether angels needed those things or not. Anyway, she hadn't finished mending the chair, yet.

When Mary eventually found her voice, all the words just fell over one another.

'Very pleased to meet you, I'm sure,' she said. 'I'm sorry that I ignored you just now, but I've just got to the tricky bit. If you want my parents, I'm afraid they're both out but if you come back about six you can see them, or of course you can talk to me but I'm sure you want someone more important. The Rabbi lives just down the road, and . . .'

'Mary! Mary!' said Gabriel. 'Let me get a word in edgeways. It's *you* I've come to see. I've been sent to tell you that God's very pleased with you. He thinks you're a very special person.'

'Oh, it's nothing really, said Mary. 'Anyone can mend a chair if they really want to.'

'Not that,' said Gabriel. 'You're going to have a baby. He's going to be a great ruler and save the world. He'll be known as the Son of God, and he'll rule for ever.'

Now if Mary hadn't known he was an angel she'd have laughed, but instead she just said, 'Me? Have a baby? That's a bit difficult for a single girl, isn't it?'

'Not for God,' said Gabriel. 'If God's decided to use you in a special way, why should he need a man to help him?'

'Well, it's usual' said Mary. 'At least where having babies is concerned.'

'Nothing's impossible for God,' said Gabriel. 'You know your cousin Elizabeth, who's never been able to have a baby?'

'Yes,' said Mary. 'Everyone thinks she's no good because of that.'

'It's certainly a very unfair world, isn't it?' said Gabriel. 'Women seem to get the blame for everything. Anyway, she's going to have a baby as well – she's six months pregnant. So don't you go saying that anything's impossible where God's concerned.'

Mary was a bit lost for words. Obviously something absolutely stunning was happening, and all she could think of to say was, 'Well, God's the boss – whatever he wants is OK by me.'

'Good,' said Gabriel. 'That's what he hoped you'd say.'

As soon as Gabriel had gone, Mary threw away the chair she was mending and all the bits fell apart again, but she was too excited to bother with mending a silly old chair! After all, any man can do that, but they can't have babies, can they! Mary went to get her coat and scarf, and then she ran out of the house and all the way to her cousin Elizabeth's place. They were so happy – they hugged one another, and they danced and sang, and were completely overjoyed. God had chosen both women for a special purpose, and no one could ever look down on either of them any more. It had always been a silly thing to do, anyway – hadn't it!

Based on Luke 1:26-40

Let's Chat

I wonder how the men felt
about being left out of things.
Perhaps they just thought
it was 'women's stuff' anyway!

We're Sad

Forgive us please, God, for silly prejudices:
for saying, 'That's a man's job',
or, 'That's women's work',
or even worse, 'That's a woman's place'!
Help us to give each other all the scope we need
to play a proper part in your work.

We're Glad

Thank you, God, for not being stuck
in the moulds we make!
Thank you for showing us
how silly they are!
Thank you for letting us be ourselves.

Let's Pray for People

Some people can't be themselves;
they always have to be
what other people expect.
Please, God, set us all free from prejudice,
and help people to live in ways that please you,
and not just each other.

There's a Baby in My Dinner!

Why are human beings so obsessed with numbers? They count everything! You wouldn't find self-respecting donkeys wasting all our time counting things. Life's too short for that. Humans, though, well they'll count anything. I know a person, not very far away, who has lots of bags full of little bits of gold. I can't see the fascination, personally – when you've seen one bit of gold you've seen them all – but he spends hours every night counting them.

Now let me see, what was I working up to? Oh, yes – the census. That's how we came to be in the silly situation I'm in now. Apparently, the government had the bright idea of counting all the people. I mean, can you imagine it? How can you count people when they won't stand still for ten minutes at a time? Well, they decided to tell them to go back to the towns where they were born and register their names; and my master, Joseph, comes from Bethlehem. Now, make no mistake, Bethlehem is a wonderful place to come from – a lousy place to go to, but wonderful to come from. Trouble was, we had to go to it. And now we're here.

To make matters worse, Joseph's wife Mary was nine months pregnant, and seemed to think that gave her the right to ride on my back everywhere. Now that's all very well, but when did you last see a pregnant donkey being given a piggyback by a human? Precisely. It's species discrimination and I intend to make a complaint about it.

Anyway, that's how we came to be here. We had a terrible journey – not a service area in sight the whole way, and the road's been neglected for years. My feet are killing me – and I've got twice as many as you have! Still, we eventually got here, and I was really looking forward to a warm stable, some soft straw and a good square meal. Well, you'll never guess. All the rooms in the hotels were full – I told Joseph he should have booked, but would he listen? The first I knew about the problem was when I was just about to lie down on the straw and in came the innkeeper and offered Joseph and Mary my room. I don't know what the world's coming to. Not only that,

but when the baby was born they put it to bed in my dinner! No kidding! Slapped it straight into the manger without so much as a 'by your leave'! Human beings really are an undeveloped species you know. I mean, we donkeys think nothing of having babies. We just get on with it, without fuss and bother, and when it's born it has to stand on its own feet – literally – straight away. These humans, though, you never saw such a carry-on. Still, I must admit there's something very special about a human baby – they're sweet little things. So naturally I wanted to have a look. I wandered over to the manger – it was meant to be for me, after all – and had a look inside. As I looked in I caught the smell of the hay, and thought I'd just get a quick nibble while I was there. You'd have thought I was doing something dreadful! Mary screamed, and Joseph got hold of my collar and started to drag me away. I tell you I'd just about had enough. What with the walk, the invasion of my privacy and now I wasn't even allowed to eat a bit of my own food. So maybe I overreacted, I don't know, but I did something that comes very naturally to us donkeys. I dug my hooves into the earth floor and refused to move an inch. Even though my feet were hurting, it was worth it. I didn't realise Joseph even knew some of the words he used! Very soon, the innkeeper and his wife came over to see what the fuss was about and I had a real live audience to play to, but they didn't stay long. The wife disappeared to the house and came back with a bucket of the most delicious-smelling oats you ever saw in your life. 'Well,' I thought, ' somebody cares about me.' Then she went and put it the other side of the stable. Of course, I knew what the game was, but I decided I'd made my point. After all, donkeys are stubborn but we're not stupid. So I walked over to the bucket and had a good feed and pretended not to notice Joseph tying me up.

We've got some visitors now, and Mary's letting them hold the baby, which gives me a chance for a good look. Mind you, I'm not too happy about the visitors – they smell of sheep and they've got little bits of wool all over their clothes. They *say* they're shepherds, and they're telling some incredible story about angels coming to them and saying that a baby had been born. They *say* that they were so excited they left their flocks in the fields and came rushing over to see the baby. They certainly look and smell like shepherds, but I know their game. I mean, what shepherd who's any good leaves the sheep in the field at night without protection? Even if they did, they wouldn't admit it to strangers.

No – I've got their number. Oh, I'll admit they're playing the part very well, right down to the grass stains on their clothes and the mud on their sandals, but I've got them rumbled. I know travelling salesmen when I see them. You mark my words, before those people leave, Mary and Joseph will have spent money they can't afford on pretty little bootees and silly cardigans with lambs all over them – now *donkeys* I could understand.

Still, even though I don't like to admit it I can see what the fuss is all about. He really does look like a pretty special baby.

(Do you think the donkey's right about the visitors?)

Based on Luke 2:1-20

Let's Chat

When Jesus comes into our lives,
things change.
And it's not always convenient!

We're Sad

We'd like to say 'sorry'
for always wanting to be comfortable
when you are trying to disturb us!
Sometimes you ask us to do things
we would rather not do,
or not to do things which we like.

We're Glad

Thank you, God,
for making life such an adventure.
Thank you for the unexpected times
when what seemed like terrible problems
turn out to be your opportunities.
Help us to be more open to you.

Let's Pray for People

Some people only ever see the hard side of life,
and don't notice the good things all round them.
That's very sad.
Please, God, help people who are unhappy
to find something to smile about,
something to give them hope.

Questions, Questions!

Joseph wasn't happy. He was tired, his head ached and his feet were sore. They were on their way home from Jerusalem, and Nazareth seemed a long, long way away. 'I don't know,' he said to Mary. 'Perhaps we ought to live a little nearer. Every year we have to make this journey for the festival – and we're not getting any younger.'

'Oh, don't start that again,' said Mary. 'We like living in Nazareth, and it *is* only once a year we have to do it. Anyway, it's always worth the effort. You must admit it was a great celebration, and Jesus loved it.'

It had been Jesus' first time at the festival. In previous years, they'd left him with his grandparents, but this year as he was twelve years old he had gone with them. He'd had a wonderful time, seeing all the sights of Jerusalem – such as the Temple and the Governor's Palace – and watching the big parades.

'Speaking of Jesus,' said Joseph, 'where is he?'

'Oh, he's with Zebedee and Rachel,' said Mary. 'You remember, he spent most of his time with them in Jerusalem.'

'Well,' said Joseph, 'he's not with them now. Look, there they are – and there's no sign of Jesus.'

Mary and Joseph weren't really worried, but they thought they'd better check, so they hurried around all the other families who were walking with them, trying to find Jesus. Gradually they realised that he simply wasn't there.

'There's nothing for it,' said Joseph. 'We'll have to go back to Jerusalem – and me with these feet.'

'Well, you can't very well go without them, can you?' said Mary, a little crossly because she was a lot more worried about Jesus than about Joseph's feet. 'Come on – the sooner we start, the sooner we'll find him. I just hope he's all right.'

So they turned round and walked all the way back again to Jerusalem. They'd already walked for a day, and could really have done with a good rest, but they were too worried to stop. On and on they walked, right through the night, with wolves howling around them and the moonlight making frightening shadows, and what with all that and being so worried about Jesus, Joseph almost forgot about his feet!

In the morning, they got to Jerusalem. 'Now where do we start looking?' wondered Joseph. 'It's a big town, and it's full of visitors!' That was true, and it seemed like a hopeless job. For three days, Joseph and Mary hunted around the city and couldn't find Jesus anywhere. They went into the hotels, they searched around the market stalls and checked all the stables, because Jesus loved animals. The only place they hadn't tried was the Temple.

'He won't be in there,' said Mary. 'After all, he's twelve years old and there are lots of things going on here that he'll find more exciting than religion.' Even so, they'd run out of ideas and thought they might as well try. So they made their way into the Temple, and straight away they noticed that quite a crowd was gathering in one of the courtyards. They pushed their way through the crowd, thinking that they might find a Temple guide who could help them to search, and guess what they saw!

In the middle of the crowd was a little circle of priests and teachers, all sitting around discussing theology. The little group were so engrossed in their talking that they didn't see Mary and Joseph pushing their way through, but Mary and Joseph had seen someone, though. Can you guess who?

There, sitting in the middle of the priests and teachers, was Jesus. He was listening very carefully to them, and asking questions. And they weren't just any old questions, either, but he was really making the wise people scratch their heads and think! Mary was embarrassed – rather like other parents often are when they think their children are being a nuisance – but was too relieved at finding Jesus safe and well to worry too much about that.

'There you are!' she said. 'What d'you think you're doing, making your father and me so worried about you? Four days we've been searching for you – and your father with his feet as well!'

Jesus looked at her, and said, 'Why did you worry? You should have known where I'd be.'

Joseph was about to say something very stern to Jesus for being cheeky to his mother, when one of the teachers spoke to Mary.

'He's your son, is he?' he said. 'Well, he's a bright lad, and he's going to go a long way.'

Yes,' said Joseph, grumpily, 'all the way back to Nazareth, and I hope his feet hurt as much as mine do.'

The teachers assured Mary and Joseph that Jesus had not been a nuisance. 'Never discourage him from asking questions,' they said. 'That's how bright children like him get even brighter.'

Mary and Joseph took Jesus home. They always remembered what the teachers had said, and encouraged Jesus to ask questions – even ones that sounded silly. And sure enough, he learned, and he became even wiser, and everyone said what a great man he was going to be one day.

Based on Luke 2:41-end.

Let's Chat

Parents wouldn't worry half so much
if they didn't love their children!

We're Sad

Sometimes we cause people who love us
to get anxious,
all because we don't think before we act.
Please, God, forgive us
and make us more considerate.

We're Glad

Thank you, God, for people who care.
Sometimes we complain about it,
tell them not to make a fuss,
or that they worry too much,
but we're glad they care enough to worry.
Thank you, God.

Let's Pray for People

Every day, people get lost, and other people worry.
Sometimes it ends happily, sometimes it doesn't.
Sometimes it seems as though it will never end at all.
Please, God, be specially close to people
who are separated from one another;
give them comfort, and hope, and if there is bad news
give them people to console them and love them,
the way you do.

Poor Ebenezer!

Ebenezer was a very careful little boy. He had decided that when he grew up he'd be rich. That was the only thing that mattered to him in the whole wide world!

He always saved as much of his pocket money as he could; he never spent it on what he thought were silly things like sweets or comics. 'After all,' he used to say, 'if you look after the pennies, the pounds will look after themselves.' The other children at school knew better than to ask him for anything. If someone wanted to borrow his pencil he would say, 'Neither a borrower nor a lender be.' And if someone was collecting for charity they never got any of Ebenezer's pocket money. Not likely! 'People should learn to look after themselves,' he used to say.

Ebenezer never had any real friends. No one seemed to want to be friends with him. Sometimes he used to be sad about that, but then he'd say to himself, 'Friends are no use. Friends don't make you rich. I'm going to be richer than all of them.'

When he was a teenager, he never seemed to have any girl friends, either. His parents got quite worried about it. 'Why don't you ask Rachel from down the road to go to the theatre with you?' his mother asked one day.

'What?' said Ebenezer. 'Have you seen the price of theatre tickets?' And he went to his bedroom to count his money. Ebenezer had quite a lot of money by now, but somehow it never seemed like very much. The trouble was that he'd got used to it. He didn't know what being rich really meant. How much do you need before people say, 'That's a rich person'? So he just thought that being rich meant having more than he had then, and that meant that he was always trying to get richer!

Gradually, the people Ebenezer had been at school with got married and started families. He used to see them sometimes, out in the front gardens of their houses playing with their children. He would have liked some children to play with, but he knew that families cost money. None of those people looked like ever being rich. So Ebenezer just had to resign himself to never having a family of his own. Instead, he bought a farm and started growing crops. 'People will always need food,' he told himself. 'I'll get really rich selling my produce to them.' And he did. But he never *felt* really rich, because 'rich' always means 'better off than I am now'!

Then one year he had a really big crop. Everything seemed to go right for Ebenezer that year. There was just the right amount of sunshine and rain, not too many slugs and snails and Ebenezer's home-made scarecrow kept the birds away. So when it came to harvest he had so much produce that he didn't know what to do with it! He had bags of wheat grain stacked up to the ceiling of his biggest barn, and so many apples, oranges and pomegranates that the greengrocers couldn't sell them fast enough. What was he to do with all this extra food?

While he was wondering, there was a knock on his door and there stood the Mayor. Ebenezer was really pleased. He'd been waiting for this for a long time. The Mayor must have come to tell him that he'd been made 'Businessman of the Year.' He'd been expecting it, of course, and he knew he deserved it because he'd made more money than everyone else

put together. This would show them! All those people who'd never wanted to be his friend would wish they'd been nicer to him, now. When he became Businessman of the Year, *everyone* would want to be his friend. But he wouldn't let them, of course. 'Too late!' he would say. 'Go away and leave me alone.' How he would enjoy seeing them squirm!

'I expect you know why I've come to see you,' the Mayor began. Ebenezer was very careful. He didn't want to look conceited.

'No,' he answered, 'I really can't imagine.'

'Well, said the Mayor, 'you've had a really terrific crop, haven't you?'

'Yes, I have,' agreed Ebenezer.

'You must be about the most successful businessman in the town,' the Mayor went on.

'What d'you mean, "about"?' thought Ebenezer. 'I'm *absolutely* the most successful businessman within a hundred miles!' He didn't say it, though, because he didn't want to sound boastful. So he just smiled modestly and nodded his head.

'So,' said the Mayor, 'We wondered whether you would consider . . .'

'Here it comes,' thought Ebenezer. 'Now I must try to look surprised.'

The Mayor continued. '. . . whether you'd consider helping out the poor people by giving some of your crops away.'

Ebenezer was just about to smile and say, 'Of course, my dear Mr Mayor! I would be honoured to accept the award,' when he realised what the Mayor had said.

'What!' he bellowed. 'You want me to give my food away? How will I ever become rich if I go doing silly things like that?'

'B-b-but you *are* rich, Ebenezer,' said the Mayor.

'Nonsense!' roared Ebenezer. 'I've got to be a lot better off than I am now, before I'm rich.'

'What are you going to do with that food, though?' asked the Mayor. 'You haven't got big enough barns to store it.'

'Then I'll build bigger ones!' said Ebenezer. 'I'll store up all the food so that I can get rich without having to work for it!' So he got some builders in and before long all his food was stored away. 'Just fancy,' he thought, 'suggesting that I should give my food away. Just because those silly people chose to have families, and wasted money on their friends, they expect me to help them when they're poor!'

That night, Ebenezer had a terrible shock. He died. No one was there to hold his hand, and no one came to his funeral to mourn for him. Poor, sad Ebenezer died as he'd lived – alone. He never got to enjoy all that lovely food, and although he had more money than everyone else in the town put together, he never thought he was rich, because to him 'rich' always meant 'better off than I am now'.

Poor, sad Ebenezer!

Based on Luke 12:16-21

Let's Chat

Why was Ebenezer always unhappy?

We're Sad

Loving God,
we're sorry for the times we've been greedy,
when we've kept more for ourselves
than we really needed
and neglected other people.
Help us to remember that it's love
that makes us truly rich.

We're Glad

God, you are our friend.
Thank you for giving us
the most important thing of all.
Thank you for your love;
help us to share it with others.

Let's Pray for People

People like Ebenezer
will never be truly happy,
because however much they have,
they just want more.
Please, God, help people to be happy
with just enough,
and help us all to discover
the joy of friendship.

AIRS AND GRACES

Tom was really excited. He had been invited to a wedding. And it wasn't just any ordinary wedding, either. It was the wedding of the famous concert pianist, Roland F. Sharpe to the operatic soprano, Edwina G. Flatte. They were a very loving couple, and everyone said how natural they were together. It was going to be a real society wedding, with all the trimmings.

Tom had hired himself a special suit for the occasion, and spent the entire morning getting ready.

'I've got to look smart,' he said. 'After all, I'm bound to be on the top table; I was an old college friend of Roland.'

'That's the first I knew of it,' said Tom's mother. 'When was that?'

'You know,' said Tom. 'During my Academy days when I was a violinist.'

'Your Academy days?' said his mother. 'You're exaggerating a bit, aren't you? And you weren't a violinist, either.'

'Yes I was,' Tom insisted.

'You worked in the canteen,' said his mother.

'I'd have been a student,' Tom protested, 'but they just didn't seem to recognise my talent.'

'Couldn't seem to find it, more likely!' his mother corrected him. 'Now, Tom, you're not going to go giving yourself airs and graces are you? I mean it's nice of Mr Sharpe to invite you at all.'

'I told you,' said Tom, 'we're real mates, old Roly and me.'

Then, without listening to any more that his mother was saying, Tom put on his coat and went out.

Meanwhile, in a different part of the town, Richard was also getting ready to go. He couldn't understand why he'd been invited. He used to work at the academy, too, as the caretaker. Although he loved music, he'd never really been able to master an instrument, but he used to sit in his office at the college listening to music on the radio, and loving every note of it. A lot of the students had very expensive instruments, which Richard used to look after for them sometimes, although it wasn't really part of his job. 'No trouble,' he used to say, 'I've got to be here anyway.' He remembered Roland Sharpe, but not very well, since Roland never used to ask him to look after his piano for him. So he couldn't imagine why he'd been invited. Still, it would be nice to see him again, now that he'd become such a success.

It was a lovely wedding; of course, the music was wonderful! All the most famous musicians were there, and Tom was having a wonderful time. After the service, he went around slapping them on the back, and talking about 'old times' with them. He thought it was rather strange that such clever people seemed to have such bad memories, but he was quite happy to remind them who he was. The only thing that really spoiled it a little was that the photographer kept on pushing him out of the camera line. He would have a word with Roly later on about that. She wouldn't keep her job long! Tom eventually decided it might be better to get off early to the reception.

Richard enjoyed the wedding, too. He sat at the back, and thought how wonderful it was to be with all these famous people. Then after the ceremony he stayed for a while, listening to the organ music, before he slipped quietly out to his car and drove to the hotel for the reception.

When Tom arrived, he was really pleased that he was such a special friend of Roly. There were so many tables! They were all set out with gleaming silver and cut glass, and the smell of the food was amazing! 'Good thing I got here ahead of them,' he thought. 'I'd better get myself a good seat.' He went to the top table and sat down near to where the couple would be.

'Better leave room for their families,' he thought. 'Don't want to be pushy.' So he chose a place a few seats away from where Roland and Edwina would sit. Very soon, the room started filling up. He couldn't think why Roly and his new wife were so late, until he caught sight of them in the doorway shaking hands with the guests. 'Oh well,' he thought, 'I can shake hands when they join me.'

Soon, he saw the happy couple approaching. Tom had his

arm around someone – oh yes, it was that caretaker fellow, Richard. Tom remembered him from his 'Academy days'. Quite a nice man, but of course not of any importance. In Tom's opinion, he was no musician – all he did was listen to it. 'Anyone could do that,' Tom used to say. 'Any fool can *listen*. What's really hard is *playing* it.' You can see now why Tom never got accepted as a student.

Roland caught sight of Tom and came straight up to him, still with his arm around Richard's shoulders. 'Hello,' he said. 'I'm sorry, but I don't think we've met.'

Tom thought it was a wonderful joke! He roared with laughter, stood up and slapped Roland on the back. 'Hi there, Roly baby!' he shouted.

'Oh, yes,' said Roland, frowning. '*Now* I remember you. Look, I'm sorry – this is rather embarrassing – this place is for

Richard here. You remember Richard, don't you. We always thought the world of him; he was so helpful – and *such* a musician! I'm sorry, but d'you mind moving? There's a place for you over there. Would you mind showing him, Richard? It's the one you were in before I found you.'

The whole room seemed to be spinning round. Tom couldn't believe what he was hearing. As Richard showed him to his seat, Tom didn't hear a word he was saying. He just had those words of Roland's ringing around inside his head. '. . . and *such* a musician.' Roland must have got confused. Yes, that was it. Poor Roland – all the pressure of fame must have got to him. Then Tom noticed that the people around him seemed to be enjoying a joke. As he passed they started giggling, and whispering to one another. Tom couldn't imagine what they were laughing at. There was nothing funny about the way he had been treated.

When he sat down, Tom watched Richard returning to the place he had wanted, and he noticed something very strange. Everyone seemed to know Richard, and to like him, and to want to talk to him. Although Richard was very shy, and found it a little embarrassing, people were grabbing his hand as he went past, and smiling as they greeted him. Tom couldn't understand it. But then, that was poor Tom's whole trouble, you see. He just couldn't understand what was really important in life, and what wasn't.

Based on Luke 14:7-11

Let's Chat

That's the problem
with putting ourselves on pedestals:
we've got further to fall!

We're Sad

It's tempting to try and pretend
that we're something we're not.
Please forgive us, God,
when we give ourselves airs and graces.
Help us just to enjoy being ourselves.

We're Glad

God, we thank you
for making us as we are.
This is how you have made us,
and you love us.
Why should we want to be anything else!

Let's Pray for People

Some people are never satisfied with themselves,
and are always pretending,
trying to impress others.
Please, God, help them to know
that you love them the way you made them.
And help us always to be kind,
and not to make people feel small
just so that we can look big.

Don't Be Taken In

Jake had a very responsible position: he was personal assistant to a man called Zebedee. Now Zebedee was so rich that he couldn't keep track of all the money he had, so it was Jake's job to do it for him. He dealt with all the accounts, and made sure that Zebedee's customers paid their bills. One evening, he was sitting in his office counting up the day's takings: 'Two for Zebedee, one for me. Two for Zebedee, one for me. Two for Zebedee, one for me,' he counted. You may think that's a very strange way to count money, but I have to tell you that Jake was not a particularly honest man, and he was taking some of Zebedee's money for himself. He always did it, and his friend Mark, who was the butler, didn't approve. 'That's Zebedee's money,' he said. 'You've got no right to take it.'

It's all right,' said Jake. 'I'm worth more than he pays me, anyway.'

'That's not the point,' persisted Mark. 'He trusts you, and if you think you deserve more you should ask him.'

'Oh go and polish your halo!' shouted Jake. Then he went on counting: 'Two for Zebedee, one for me. Two for Zebedee, one for me.'

Mark went away, but he was very angry. 'Zebedee's a good boss,' he thought. 'He was really kind to me when I was in trouble. I can't stand by and see him being cheated by someone he trusts.'

Now this was very difficult for Mark. He didn't like people who gossiped, but the more he thought about it the more convinced he was that he had to tell Zebedee.

'I hope you don't think I'm prying,' he said, 'but do you actually know how much money you've got?'

'Well it's not really your business, is it?' said Zebedee. 'Anyway, I leave all that to Jake.'

'That's the point,' said Mark. 'I don't like telling you this, but if I were you I'd do a bit of checking up.'

Zebedee was not pleased, and he sent for Jake. 'I don't know exactly what's been going on,' he said, 'but I mean to find out. I've got to go away for a few days, and when I come back, you and I are going to go through the books together. Anything wrong with them and you'll be looking for a new job.'

'Oh dear!' thought Jake. 'What am I going to do? I'm no good at heavy work, and I'm far too proud to beg. Whatever am I going to do?' Then he had an idea.

While Zebedee was away, Jake sent messages to everyone who owed Zebedee money, saying that if they came to see him he would help them. So early in the morning there was quite a queue of people outside Jake's office. The first one in was a farmer called Luke.

'Tell me,' Jake asked, 'just how much is it that you owe Zebedee?'

'Er – I'm afraid it's rather a lot,' Luke answered. 'I owe him for a thousand gallons of olive oil.'

'My word!' said Jake. 'That's an awful lot of olive pips! Look, I'll tell you what, let's call it five hundred.'

Luke was amazed. 'Are you sure that's all right?' he asked.

'Oh yes,' replied Jake airily. 'I'm in charge around here.'

'Well,' said Luke, 'it's very kind of you I'm sure. If ever there is anything you need – anything at all – you just ask me and I'll help you.'

'Thank you,' said Jake. 'I'll be sure to remember.'

Jake called the next person in. This was the local baker, called Sam, and he was very worried. 'Look, I know I owe you for that wheat,' he said, 'but you know how it is, and money doesn't buy what it used to – and then there was the yeast shortage last month – it sent the price sky high; and my flour grinders have just gone on strike for better pay and free bread. I'm terribly sorry, but I simply can't pay you.'

'Exactly how much wheat do you owe for?' asked Jake.

'A hundred kilogrammes of it, I'm afraid,' Sam replied, 'but with all the competition from cheap imported bread I'm just not doing the trade.'

'Don't worry,' said Jake. 'Let's call it fifty kilogrammes – would that help?'

'Oh, ever so much!' said Sam. 'I'm really very grateful. And my wife will be, too – did I tell you she'd been ill? The medical bills have been crippling! Anyway – if I can ever help you at all, you only have to ask.'

Can you see what Jake was up to?

The next person in was Dave. He was a caterer and he did most of the weddings and other big events in the neighbourhood. He wasn't at all happy about the wine bill he'd been sent.

'These prices are ridiculous!' said Dave. 'All that money for a few casks of wine – I'm not paying that!'

'I don't think you'd get it cheaper anywhere else,' said Jake.

'You must be kidding!' said Dave. 'Why, at one of the weddings I did, we ran out of wine and a guest made some more out of plain water. True as I'm standing here. Now if he can do that, how come you have to charge so much?'

'Well, I'll tell you what,' said Jake. 'Why don't we just mark your account as paid?'

Dave was quite taken aback by that. He'd come here looking for a fight, and now he wasn't getting one! He couldn't think of anything to say, except, 'Hmm! Well! Very good, I'm sure. Let me know if I can help you any time.'

'Oh, don't worry,' Jake answered him. 'I shall.'

This went on all day, and before long Jake had lots and lots of friends in the town. So when Zebedee came back he wasn't too worried. He knew Zebedee was going to give him the sack, but he thought he'd get in first.

'I've decided to leave,' he said. 'You'll find your affairs are all quite in order.'

'I doubt that very much,' said Zebedee, 'but since you're leaving we'll say no more about it. I didn't really want a scene, anyway. You're a rogue and a cheat, but for some reason I find it hard to stay angry with you.'

So Jake left. He hadn't got a job to go to straight away, but he never starved because he'd managed to convince all the people in the town that he was a wonderfully nice man, and they all loved him and wanted to help him out. Everybody, that is, except Mark who knew exactly what had been going on. One day, Mark was talking to Luke, who said, 'Smashing chap, that Jake – really helped me out when I was in trouble.'

Well,' said Mark, 'he's certainly clever, I'll grant you that. But if I've got the choice between a clever person and an honest one, give me the honest one every time.'

And I think he was right.

What about you?

Based on Luke 16:1-9

Let's Chat

Jake was a very clever man,
but would you want him for a friend?

We're Sad

Sometimes, God,
we think we're really clever
when we pull the wool over people's eyes.
We're sorry for being dishonest;
please forgive us, and help us
to earn the trust of others.

We're Glad

However many times we get things wrong,
you will never send us away.
Thank you, God, for loving us so much,
and for forgiving us so often.

Let's Pray for People

We pray for people
who are afraid of losing their jobs.
Please, God, help them to trust you
and not resort to dishonest tricks.

BEN AND NEB GET BETTER

I want to introduce you to two friends called Ben and Neb. Neb had been named after a famous Persian king, who had a very long name that no one could pronounce properly – so they just shortened it to Neb. Although Ben and Neb were great friends, they were as opposite as their names. They weren't from the same part of the country, either. Ben was from Galilee while Neb was from the next county, called Samaria, and as a rule the people of those two counties liked each other about as much as supporters of Manchester United and Aston Villa! They each thought the other worshipped the wrong God – again, a bit like supporters of Manchester United and Aston Villa! So how did Ben and Neb come to be friends? Well now, there's something I haven't told you about them. They weren't very nice to look at, because they had a very unpleasant disease which made them come out in a rash all over. Everybody was afraid of catching it, and so they drove Ben and Neb away. They didn't belong anywhere, and they lived right on the border between the two counties so that whenever anybody started throwing stones at them they could just nip across the border and get away. Of course, it got a bit difficult if people from both counties were doing it at the same time!

Anyway, even though they were from rival gangs, as it were, the fact that both of them had been kicked out of their gangs mean't they actually got on together quite well!

One day, Ben and Neb met up with some other people like themselves. There were eight of them (you don't want to know all their names – it would take far too long) and they all had nasty rashes just like Ben and Neb had. They thought it was really unfair that people treated them badly just because they didn't look very nice, and they'd decided to do something about it. One of them, whose name was Rachel, said, 'We've heard about a man called Jesus who heals people, and we're going to find him. They say he's in these parts.' Ben and Neb thought that anything was worth a try – so they joined up with

Rachel and her friends. After a few days, they saw a man walking along the road towards them with a lot of other people around him. Rachel knew that Jesus always travelled with other people, so she thought this might be him. Then she saw some faces she knew. 'That's Levi,' she said. 'He was pestering me for my taxes, but I got away without paying any.'

'How did you do that?' asked Ben

'I offered him the money with my bad hand,' replied Rachel, 'and he was so horrified he wouldn't take it! Anyway, I heard he'd joined up with Jesus.'

'Jesus is not going to want to know us,' said Ben. 'Look, he's got all his friends round him.'

'From what I've heard,' Rachel answered, 'he isn't worried about what people think. I had a friend called Joe once, who was worse than any of us, and Jesus touched him.'

'You're the one that's touched,' said Ben, 'if you believe tales like that! No one touches people like us.'

'You can scoff if you like,' Rachel answered him, 'but it's true. Joe told me himself, but by the time I'd got over the shock Jesus had gone – and I've been looking for him ever since.'

Neb thought it was worth trying, anyway. 'Why don't we just shout to him from where we are?' he suggested. 'Then if he doesn't want to get too close he can say so.'

'Fair enough,' said Rachel, and she started shouting. 'Hey, Jesus! over here! Can you help us?'

Jesus called back, 'Go and show yourselves to the priests.' That was because in those days the priests were very important, and they had to say it was okay for people who'd been chased away to come back.

Ben was disappointed. 'Fat lot of good that is!' he said. 'It's the priests who put us here in the first place. If we go back without being cured first, they'll just chase us away again.'

They didn't know what to do next. It seemed obvious that Jesus wasn't going to help them.

'I don't understand it,' said Rachel. 'It's not like Jesus to send people away.' Then her eyes lit up. There was something else she'd heard about Jesus. Apparently, Jesus had this saying he used to use a lot (most people have their own pet sayings, but the ones Jesus used actually meant something): 'Your faith has made you well.' So perhaps that was what Jesus was up to!

'Come on,' said Rachel. 'Let's go.'

'Don't be silly,' said Ben. 'There's no point.'

'Yes there is,' said Rachel. 'Trust me!' Then she thought for a moment and said, 'Sorry – I meant trust Jesus.' And off she went towards the city.

Gradually, one by one the other nine shrugged their shoulders and followed. As they were walking along, though, Ben started thinking. 'I bet Jesus is having a good laugh at us,' he said. The more he thought about it, the more angry he became until he could keep quiet no longer. He went up to Rachel and started shouting at her about how silly and how humiliating it all was. 'And if you think I'm going to let Jesus make a fool of me,' he yelled, wagging his finger in Rachel's face, 'you've got another think coming.'

Rachel wasn't listening to Ben; she was staring at the finger that was being waved in front of her. 'Hey, Ben!' she shouted. 'Look at your finger!'

Don't change the subject!' shouted Ben who was really wound up now.

'No, really!' said Rachel. 'Look – the skin's healthy. And your face as well.'

Ben stopped yelling and looked. It was true. His hands and arms were healthy as though he'd been given a completely new skin. Then he said to Rachel, 'Your face is better, too.' And before long, they were all jumping up and down for joy, because they realised they had been healed.'

'Come on,' said Rachel. 'Let's go to the priests.'

'Shouldn't we go and thank Jesus, first?' asked Neb, but Rachel and the others were too excited to listen.

'Oh, he'll be long gone by now,' said Rachel.

'That's true,' said Ben. 'Anyway, the priests are far more important than Jesus is.'

So off they went – or at least, nine of them did. Neb just said, 'I'll catch up with you later,' and went to find Jesus. When he found him he went rushing up to say thank you.

Jesus turned to his disciples, and said, 'Isn't that interesting? Ten were healed, but only one says thank you – and he's the last one you'd have expected to. You know, the people who are called "outsiders" are often the ones with real faith.'

Based on Luke 17:11-19

Let's Chat

How important is it to say 'Thank you'?
How often do we all forget?
(That's including grown ups!)

We're Sad

People are often very kind to us,
and we don't notice.
Or sometimes we notice
but forget to say 'Thank you'.
We're sorry, God. Please forgive us,
and teach us to appreciate each other.

We're Glad

We often hear what a dreadful world this is,
but it's still full of wonderful people!
Sometimes, we get kindnesses,
or perhaps appreciation,
from people from whom we don't expect it.
Thank you, God, for lovely surprises!

Let's Pray for People

Some people suffer from diseases
which other people find frightening.
So they get pushed away and feel lonely.
Please, God, help us to be kind to people
who need friendship most,
and help us not to be afraid.

Keep Your Wig On, Judge!

Gabriella's husband had died and she was left alone with her daughter, Becky. In those days women's jobs were not very well paid at all, and even if she could get a good job Gabriella couldn't leave Becky on her own while she went to work. So how were they going to pay the rent?

Sam, the landlord, had always seemed a nice man. That was when Gabriella's husband was alive, though – when the rent was being paid each week. Sam was one of those people who was always very nice to anyone who had money to spend, but changed completely if they fell on hard times. So when Gabriella went to see him he was not very helpful.

'It's not my fault you husband's dead, is it?' he said, nastily. 'I've still got to live you know. I've got to pay my butler, and the man who prunes my roses, and of course I only drink the very best wine. So I can't go reducing people's rent or I might end up poor and pathetic like you.'

Gabriella was really upset. 'I thought you were a friend,' she cried.

'Look, sister,' sneered Sam, 'there are no friends in business. And this is business. You find the money, or I'll find another tenant – one who won't whinge all the time.'

Gabriella didn't know what to do. She was really angry with Sam, but she knew that if she didn't find the money then she and Becky would have nowhere to live. So she tried to earn the money. For a time she got a job fruit picking, but she knew that once the season was over that would come to an end. Then she heard about a job as a cleaner at the local tailor's. The work was quite hard – Gabriella was always getting hurt by needles and scissors that were left lying around – and it was very badly paid. Also, she had to take Becky along with her, and she didn't think that was either safe or fair.

One day Becky said to her mother, 'If you didn't have to pay so much rent, you wouldn't need to earn so much money.'

Gabriella smiled. How wonderful it must be to be a child, and to see everything in such simple ways, she thought. If only

Becky knew what a complicated world it really was! 'The trouble is,' she explained, 'that Sam owns most of the houses in the town and so he can charge what he likes.'

That afternoon, when they were out for a walk, they saw a man who was wearing really funny clothes. Becky thought he looked silly – especially since he was wearing a wig. 'Hasn't he got any hair of his own?' she asked.

'Yes,' laughed Gabriella, 'but he's a very important person. He's a judge.'

'Oh,' said Becky. 'Does that mean that the more important people are, the more silly they have to look?'

Gabriella thought that Becky might have a point, but she was teaching her daughter to be polite, so she said, 'You mustn't talk like that about people. He probably thinks that your clothes are silly, but he hasn't said so.'

'What does a judge do, then?' asked Becky.

'Oh,' said her mother, 'he settles arguments between people. If someone's being unfair to someone else then he can tell them to stop.'

Before Gabriella could stop her, Becky was running over to the judge.

'Hey, mister Judgy person,' she called out. 'Can you help my mum, please, and stop Sam charging her so much rent – and I promise I won't say your wig looks silly ever again.'

The judge, who knew just how important he was and wanted everyone else to know it as well, stopped and looked first at Becky and then at Gabriella. 'Is this abominable child your responsibility?' he shouted. 'Take her home and punish her – and teach her to be polite to important people, you disgusting, scruffy woman.'

'She's not abominable,' said Gabriella, 'and if I'm scruffy it's because I do an honest job. Anyway, I'd rather be scruffy than rude and arrogant. Come on, Becky.'

Gabriella was surprised at herself. Who would ever have thought that she would speak to a judge like that? 'I shouldn't have done that,' she said to Becky. 'We must always be polite. Just because someone's rude to you doesn't mean you can be rude back.'

'You weren't rude,' said Becky. 'You were just standing up for yourself. Anyway, I think he should help you.'

Gabriella started thinking about what Becky had said. Perhaps she should go and see the judge.

'Why should I help you?' the judge said. 'You're the rude woman with the horrible child, aren't you?'

'I'm sorry if you think I was rude,' said Becky, 'but you weren't very polite, either. Anyway what you think of me doesn't alter the case. I'm being charged too much rent.'

'Go away,' said the Judge. 'Sam is a good respectable citizen. And he's very rich. We need rich people in this town a lot more than we need characters like you.'

That did it. Gabriella decided the judge was going to do the right thing, if it took her the rest of her life to make him do it. Every day, she went to his house and knocked on his door, but he wouldn't see her. Then she made a big poster saying, 'Sack the unjust judge' and went and stood outside his courtroom with it. Soon she was joined by other women, and every time the judge went past they started chanting, 'Fair rents for all'.

Eventually, it all got too much for the judge, and he called Sam to see him at his courtroom.

'You'll have to lower your rents,' he said.

'Not me,' said Sam. 'Anyway, if I do that, I'll have less to pay you.'

'Shut up!' hissed the judge. 'Do you want the whole town to hear? Look, I've had enough of being pestered by these women. Either you reduce your rents or we'll get the inspectors in to check your houses over.'

'Oh, don't do that!' said Sam, hastily. 'I'll cut the rents.'

The judge went and told the women. 'Now will you leave me alone?' he asked.

'Well,' said Gabriella, 'we're very pleased about the rents, but we think we ought to talk to you about fair wages for cleaners.'

Based on Luke 18:2-5

Let's Chat

Some people have to be pestered
to do anything!
It's a good thing God isn't like that!

We're Sad

Sometimes, we're a bit like that judge:
we know what we should do,
but we try to get out of it.
Please forgive us, God,
and make us more willing to help people.

We're Glad

Thank you, God, for not having to be pestered.
Thank you for listening to us,
and for caring about us.

Let's Pray for People

There are lots of people like Gabriella,
who have to fight for fair treatment.
Loving God, please help us to care more,
and to make the world more fair
without waiting to be pestered into it.

NONCOMMITTAL NICK

There was a man called Nicodemus who was a member of the Jewish Council – a bit like being a Member of Parliament today. Well, Nicodemus was a real politician – he thought he could talk his way through life with no problem. He prided himself on always being able to see both sides of a question, which is generally a good thing. What he couldn't understand, though, was that even if you see both sides, you sometimes have to make a choice. You can't go on for ever trying to face in two directions at once.

Nicodemus was very proud of being on the Council – after all, not everybody could achieve that. He had a lot of power, and people respected him. Well, they acted as though they did if they were sensible – after all, they never knew when they might need a powerful friend. So Nicodemus enjoyed going around the town in his fine councillor's clothes and seeing people smile at him and move out of his way. He liked the Council meetings as well, when they used to discuss all kinds of things that they thought were terribly important, and use words that they thought no one else could understand. That really made them all feel superior.

Nicodemus knew about Jesus. He'd seen him and his friends walking around, and he'd heard him teach a few times – and he and his friends on the Council were rather worried. What Jesus said seemed to make sense, and they had a sneaking feeling that he was the special person God had promised to send to save the world. So they should have been pleased, but there was something they didn't like.

Jesus was going around saying that being rich and powerful wasn't important. He said it was how you treated other people that really mattered to God. He seemed to want everyone to care about poor people. Worse than that, he wanted them to share with horrible, dirty people – and with people who had dreadful diseases that might be catching. Of course, Nicodemus felt sorry for those people, but he didn't think he could ever hug them the way Jesus did. Still, he was so impressed by Jesus that he decided to go and see him, and try to come to an arrangement. 'I'd better go at night,' he thought. 'I don't want my friends knowing I've been to see Jesus – they might think I'm one of his followers.'

So it was that late one evening when Jesus was enjoying the night air, along came Nicodemus. Now Nicodemus was a politician – so he thought he knew how to get round people. 'Excuse me, Jesus,' he said. 'I do hope I'm not bothering you but you're such a good and clever person – and we know you must be God's special worker because you do the most wonderful, amazing, simply superfantapendous things . . .'

'Oh dear!' thought Jesus. 'A politician – you can always tell them.' So he came straight to the point. 'If you want to follow me,' he said, 'it'll mean a complete change of life. Like being born all over again.'

Nicodemus thought that sounded really weird. 'What?' he said. 'I'm a bit big for that now you know.'

'I'm telling you the truth,' Jesus said. 'You've got to change so much that you leave the old life behind – just like being born again. You can't compromise on this one.'

Now I don't know about you, but I think Nicodemus understood exactly what Jesus was saying, but we've all done the same, haven't we? If we don't want to do what somebody's asking, it's easiest to say that we don't understand. And I think that's what Nicodemus was doing. So Jesus spelled it out for him.

'Look, Nicodemus,' he said, 'the world can offer you

wonderful things: power, money, influence. But none of that lasts for ever – and neither does your life. If you want the really important things – things that *do* last for ever – the world can't give you those. Only God can. That's why you can't compromise. Go on, Nicodemus – let God change your life! Let him give you life that lasts for ever.'

'That sounds wonderful,' said Nicodemus. 'What do I have to do?'

'Just let go,' said Jesus. 'Stop trying to hang onto all the money and power. Stop worrying about what your friends will think or whether you'll be able to afford nice clothes. Let go of all that, and let God change your life.'

'Well, I'd like to of course,' said Nicodemus, 'but it's not that simple. I've got a family, and a big house with a mortgage to pay on it. And I'm someone who's respected in the neighbourhood. People come to me for advice, or to help them if they're in trouble. I'm a man of position. You can't expect me to give all that up.'

'That's the point,' said Jesus. 'Life with God is never clear-cut and easy. It's like the wind. You hear it blowing, but you never quite know where it's come from or where it's going. That's how it is with the life God gives.'

Nicodemus was unhappy. He really thought Jesus and his friends had a better kind of life than he did, for all his money and power. He could see that what Jesus was doing really meant something. And in his heart of hearts he really did care about the people Jesus helped. But he just couldn't bring himself to do what Jesus was asking. 'After all,' he thought, 'what's wrong with a bit of compromise? If I keep my money and my position, I can help those poor people – but it doesn't mean I've got to be one of them.'

So Nicodemus went sadly on his way. And Jesus stood there, just as sadly, and watched him go. After all, God doesn't want to force anybody to live his life – even though it would be wonderful if everyone did!

That wasn't the end of the story for Nicodemus. He carried on battling with himself for a long time before he finally made his choice.

Poor old Noncommittal Nick!

Based on John 3:1-8

Let's Chat

Anyone can be noncommittal,
and most of us are
for at least part of the time.

We're Sad

We're sorry, God,
for the times when we refuse
to commit ourselves
because we're afraid it might be difficult.
Give us the courage to do
what we believe to be right.

We're Glad

You're never noncommittal, God!
You always commit yourself to us,
and sometimes it causes you a lot of pain.
Thank you for always being committed.

Let's Pray for People

It's so easy to get trapped
by wealth, or by our own importance,
or by fear of what others might say.
We pray for people who would like
to be committed to you,
but are afraid of what they might lose.
Please help them to be brave.

Breakfast on the Beach

Peter was fed up. He should have been very happy, because Jesus had risen from the dead, but he was fed up. That's how life sometimes is; when we should be feeling really happy about some big thing that's happened, something much less serious makes us feel down. Isn't it strange?

The reason Peter was unhappy was that he and his friends had been out in their boat fishing all night and hadn't caught anything. That wouldn't have been so bad if John hadn't been there to make fun of him. 'What's the matter, Peter? Your ugly mug frightening the fish, is it?' he asked.

Peter was about to make a sarcastic reply when he heard another voice. 'Have you caught anything?'

'Who was that?' asked Peter.

'It was that guy on the beach,' said Thomas. 'I can't see who he is.'

Peter shouted back, 'Not a blooming thing!'

'Try the other side of the boat,' called the man on the beach.

Peter wasn't impressed. 'What does he know?' he said scornfully. 'Just some landlubber out walking his dog, I expect.'

'I don't know,' replied John. 'Perhaps he can see something from where he is that we can't. We might as well give it a try.'

So they hauled the net in, with Peter grumbling about wasting time and energy, and threw it over the other side of the boat. Peter was just saying, 'With our luck we might have been just about to catch something when we hauled the net up,' when the net got terribly heavy. It was full of fish – more than they had ever caught before. In fact there were so many that they couldn't get the net into the boat.

'I know who that is!' said John. 'It's Jesus – I've seen him do that before!'

Without another word, Peter was over the side of the boat and wading to the shore, he was so excited at seeing Jesus. 'That's right,' grumbled John. 'Leave us to do the hard work, why don't you?'

When they got the boat to the shore, they emptied the net

on the beach. 'Look!' said Thomas. 'There's every kind of fish you can think of in here!' And so there was.

'Yes,' replied Jesus, 'and the net hasn't broken. There's room for all different kinds as far as I'm concerned.'

John was sure that must mean something, but he was too happy at seeing Jesus to stop and work it out. 'That will keep for later,' he thought.

Meanwhile, Jesus had got a nice warm fire going. Peter was drying himself in front of it, and Jesus took some of the fish they had caught and started to cook breakfast. John had never quite got used to the way Jesus always seemed to want to do things for them. 'He's the boss,' he used to think. '*We* should be doing the work.' But Jesus always said that being the leader meant serving others, not wanting them to serve you. It was going to take his friends a long time to learn that one – and quite a lot of us are still learning it!

After breakfast, Jesus said to Peter, 'Simon, son of John, are you my best friend?'

Peter didn't like the sound of that. Why had Jesus gone back to his old name? Jesus had given him a new name, 'Peter: the Rock' – a sign of how strong he was. Why had he started calling him Simon? Through a mouthful of fish, he said, 'Of course I am – you know that.'

'Then look after my other friends,' said Jesus.

Peter thought this was very odd. Of course he'd look after Jesus' friends – except when Jesus was around to do it himself, of course!

Then Jesus asked him again, 'Simon, son of John, are you my friend?'

By now, Peter had added some bread to the fish in his mouth – he'd never learned to eat sensibly – so it was quite difficult to speak, but he said again, 'Of course I am, Jesus. You know I'm your friend.'

'Then take care of the others,' said Jesus.

Peter was getting quite puzzled by now, and then Jesus made it even worse by asking him again, 'Simon, son of John, are you my friend?'

Peter didn't like the sound of all this at all. What was Jesus getting at? 'Of course, I am!' he shouted. 'You know perfectly well that I am.'

'Then care for the rest,' said Jesus.

Peter was getting thoroughly confused. Why all this 'Simon son of John' stuff? You don't talk to your friends in that formal way! And why had Jesus asked three times? Then he realised. Just a few days earlier, Peter had been very frightened, and had pretended not to know Jesus. And he hadn't done it just once. He'd done it – can you guess? – yes, three times. And to make matters worse, Jesus had caught him at it! So now Jesus had made him say three times that he was his friend. And he'd told him not to let the rest down the way he had *him*. Peter was very ashamed, and very sad.

'Don't let it get you down, Peter,' said Jesus, quietly. 'If you don't face up to things you can't deal with them. But now it's all behind you, and you'll be stronger from now on. You'll need to be, because things are going to get rough.'

Peter didn't like the sound of that, but he thought it was just like Jesus to make him face up to things he'd rather have avoided. 'Being a friend of his isn't a fairy tale,' he thought, 'but then, he's a *real* friend!'

They tidied up the breakfast things, to leave the beach nice and clean, and started to walk away. Peter was still thinking hard, and still a little bit angry about being singled out (although he really knew why Jesus had done it) and suddenly he pointed his finger at John and shouted out to Jesus, 'All right then; what about him? What's he going to do?'

Jesus looked at Peter very patiently. 'Never mind what he's going to do,' he said. 'That's none of your business. Why, even if I asked him to wait here until I came back – even then, it would still be no concern of yours, would it?'

That did it! Before long there was a rumour flying around that John was never going to die. But that wasn't what Jesus had said at all, was it!

Based on John 21:1-23

Let's Chat

We are friends of Jesus,
and he will forgive us anything!

We're Sad

Jesus, you love us so much
and still we let you down.
Sometimes we behave as though
we don't even know you.
Please forgive us.

We're Glad

Wonderful, loving friend,
thank you for being so patient
and so forgiving toward us.
Thank you for loving us so much.

Let's Pray for People

Some people feel very guilty,
and think they can never be forgiven.
Jesus, you were let down by your best friend.
Help people to know that if you could forgive *him*,
then you can forgive anybody.

Wait for the Power

The friends of Jesus were wondering what to do. Jesus had gone back to heaven, and left them to carry on his work, but he'd told them not to start straight away. 'Stay in Jerusalem,' he had said, 'until you get the power you need.' So they were waiting, all together, in a secret meeting room.

Peter was getting impatient, though. 'It's all very well,' he said, 'but the city is full of people. We shan't have another chance like this for nearly a year. We should be telling people about Jesus.'

'Jesus told us to wait,' said Matthew, who used to be a tax collector before he met Jesus. 'I know all about that – people used to keep me waiting for months.'

'It's no good, anyway,' said James. 'The visitors are from all over the world – we'd need to know dozens of different languages if we were going to tell them about Jesus.'

'Let's be honest,' said Thomas. 'We don't really want to go out there, anyway. There are people who want to kill us, and I'm too young to die – come to think of it, I always will be.'

As usual, Thomas was the most honest one of the group; he was saying what the others were afraid to say. And as usual, he got into trouble for it.

'I'm not afraid of anyone out there!' said Peter. 'I'll soon show them . . .' But his voice tailed off – Petered out, you might say – because he'd remembered how he used to say that to Jesus, but when it actually came to it he'd lost his nerve. It was easy to talk big among friends, but very different to have faith, and be brave when things got dangerous! 'Well, anyway,' he mumbled, 'Jesus told us to wait.'

In their hearts, everybody knew that Thomas was right. That was why they'd bolted the doors and not told anyone else where they were. The friends of Jesus were good people, and good friends – but they had reason to be afraid; the people who had killed Jesus were now looking for his followers, and they weren't going to invite them to tea! Most people would be just as frightened as they were if they had to face that kind of thing.

The problem was, though, how were they ever going to get the courage to do Jesus' work? They had seen him several times after he had risen from the dead, and yet they still seemed to be frightened of being killed themselves. How could that ever be changed? No wonder they were a little bit glum!

Just as they were beginning to get desperate, and thinking what dreadful, useless disciples they were, they heard a strange sound. 'Close the window, Andrew,' said John. 'Sounds like the wind's getting up.'

'It's already closed,' said Andrew. 'We barred it up to keep the religious leaders out so that they can't hurt us.'

'Well you didn't do it properly,' grumbled Peter. 'That's the trouble with you – you can't be trusted.'

'Ooh! Look who's talking!' said Andrew, and he would have said a lot more but Thomas stopped him.

'It's not the wind,' he said. 'I can't feel any draught at all. Something funny's going on here.'

All the disciples sat very quietly and listened. Sure enough, the noise got louder and louder, but they couldn't feel the wind. Thomas was just thinking that it was a bit like the burning bush, when Moses had seen the flames but the bush didn't actually burn, when he noticed flames as well.

'Hey, Peter!' he said. 'Your hair's on fire!'

'Don't be daft!' said Peter. 'I'd know if my hair was on fire. You're the one who's got that problem.'

Then they realised that there seemed to be flames over everybody's head. 'It *is* like the burning bush!' thought Thomas. 'Something special's happening.'

'Come on!' shouted Peter. 'Let's go outside and . . .' But he was too late. They'd gone. They'd unbolted the door and gone rushing out into the street and started telling everyone that Jesus was alive – and all of a sudden they were language experts! Andrew was speaking in Persian to a group of carpet merchants, while John had cornered a couple of soldiers and was talking in Latin, and Thomas – who had always doubted the importance of learning languages – was busy winning an argument with some philosophers, in Greek.

Then Peter realised what he was doing. 'This is silly,' he thought. 'We could get ourselves into serious trouble doing this.' He realised he was still quite frightened, but then he thought, 'Well some things are worth getting into trouble for – and there's nothing more important than doing this.'

That morning, thousands of people heard the good news that Jesus was alive. The religious authorities didn't like it. 'What will happen to all our power and our privileges,' they asked, 'if ordinary people start being listened to?' So they went around saying that Peter and his friends were drunk.

'Do me a favour!' laughed Peter. 'At this time of the morning? This is the power of God at work, but you're too bothered about yourselves to recognise it.'

Then the disciples realised that this was the 'power' Jesus had promised them. They knew there would still be hard and dangerous times ahead because Jesus had told them that, too. But they knew it was worth it. Now they understood that, whatever happened, Jesus would always be with them and God wouldn't let their lives or their work be wasted.

Now that's what I call power!

Based on Acts 2:1-21

Let's Chat

The gift of language!
The Holy Spirit helped very different people
to understand one another!

We're Sad

Sometimes it's difficult to understand
people who are different from us,
but that's no reason not to try.
Please, God, forgive us
for letting differences keep us apart.

We're Glad

Holy Spirit,
you break down all the barriers
between different people.
Thank you for making it possible
for us to listen to one another.

Let's Pray for People

We pray for the world,
full of many different kinds of people,
speaking different languages,
and even using the same language differently.
Please, God, give us the gift of understanding,
and stop us being afraid of each other.

A Disciple in the Desert

Jim was a very important man; he was one of the advisers to the queen of Ethiopia. In fact, he was one of the chief advisers. Whenever the queen had to make a really important decision, Jim was one of the people she asked for advice. This was partly because he knew an awful lot about the rest of the world. He understood the customs and the religious beliefs of other countries, and he could always see things from other people's point of view – and that's something that all really important people ought to be able to do.

One day, Jim went to the queen and said, 'I'd like to go to the Jerusalem festival this year, Your Majesty, if you could give me some time off.'

The queen wasn't really very happy about it, because she didn't want to have to do without her most trusted adviser; but she knew that as well as enjoying the festival Jim would probably learn a lot, and be an even better adviser than he was already. So she let him go, but she sent a servant with him to make sure he was well looked after and said, 'Don't stay too long – I might need you here.'

Jim had a wonderful time at the festival, but he remembered the queen's words and after a few days he knew he had to go home, although the festival was still in full swing. Before he set out for home, though, there was one more thing he had to do: buy himself a souvenir.

Meanwhile, also in Jerusalem was Philip, who was one of Jesus' friends. Jesus had gone back to heaven a few weeks before, but his friends knew that he was still with them, although they couldn't see him. He'd promised that when he left. 'I will always be with you,' he'd said, 'until the end of time.' So Philip was wondering whether there was anything particular that Jesus wanted him to do, when he had a strange idea that he ought to go for a walk along the Gaza Road.

Now Gaza Road was called by that name for a very good reason: because it led to Gaza. On the way, though, it went through the desert and that was not a very nice place to be.

Philip thought it would be much nicer to stay in Jerusalem where there was good company, plenty of food and drink, and parties going on all the time. After all, he thought, who wants to leave Jerusalem during the festival? There again, one can have too much of parties, and perhaps the walk and a bit of quiet would do him good. So he told Andrew where he was going and set off toward Gaza.

At about the time Philip set off, Jim was still looking for his souvenir. He didn't like Jerusalem rock very much, as it was hard and not very tasty; 'Fine for building temples on,' Jim used to say, 'but you can't eat it.' And he'd always thought that chariot stickers saying 'I've been to Jerusalem' were rather silly, so he looked around for something more special. 'I know,' he thought. 'I'll buy myself a Bible. It will remind me of my visit, and I'll have something to read on the journey home.' So he bought his Bible and went back to where his servant was keeping an eye on the chariot. 'That's it,' he said. 'We can go home now. You drive, Josh, and I'll have a read.'

As it happened, Jim opened his Bible at a story called *The Suffering Servant.* He felt very sorry for this servant who seemed to be having a really hard time, but he was also puzzled. 'Who is this person?' he thought.

Just as they got out into the desert, Josh called out, 'There's some chap walking on the road. Do you think he's lost?'

Jim was going to say, 'Stop and see if we can help,' when the man turned and walked towards them.

'Good morning!' said Philip, 'Are you enjoying your book?'

'Yes, very much,' answered Jim. 'But I don't really understand it.'

'I think I can probably explain it to you,' said Philip.

'Oh, that's wonderful!' said Jim. 'If you're going my way, why not hop in?'

'I'm always going your way,' said Philip, which Jim thought was rather a strange thing to say. Josh started driving again while Philip and Jim read together.

'What I want to know,' said Jim, 'is whether this writer is writing about himself or somebody else.'

'It's a prophecy,' Philip explained. 'And it's only recently come true. It's about Jesus who loved people so much that he died for them.' Then Philip went on and told Jim all about his friend Jesus, who had died, risen again and gone back to heaven, but had promised always to be with them.

Jim thought it was a wonderful story. 'How do I become a friend of Jesus, like you?' he asked.

'Be baptised,' Philip answered. 'It's a sign that you want to make a new start – like being washed clean.'

Just at that moment, they were passing an oasis, and Jim said, 'Well, here's some water, so you can baptise me now.' He told Josh to stop the chariot, and he and Philip got out and went into the water. Josh thought they must have gone mad, but he didn't say anything – after all, even friends of Jesus could lose their tempers, and Jim was a powerful man!

After Philip had baptised Jim, they came out of the water and dried themselves off. Philip was wondering what he should do next, because he had travelled a long way in the chariot and although he liked walking he didn't fancy that long a walk, especially in the desert sun. Jim had thought of that, and was going to offer to run Philip back, but suddenly Philip wasn't there any more. God had whisked him off somewhere else – there were still lots of other people who wanted to hear about Jesus.

Jim carried on toward Ethiopia. On the way he read the story of *The Suffering Servant* again. He found it had a whole new meaning because of what he'd been told about Jesus. When he arrived back, the queen was very pleased to see him.

'Did you have a good time in Jerusalem?' she asked.

'Oh yes, thank you, Your Majesty,' answered Jim. 'But the really exciting part happened on the way back.'

Based on Acts 8:26-39

Let's Chat

Philip must have wondered
where on earth God was sending him!
I bet he'd rather have stayed in Jerusalem.

We're Sad

Sometimes, God, you ask us
to go to places we'd rather not.
Please forgive us for the times
when we have been unwilling to go.

We're Glad

We want to say thank you, God,
for people who have gone out of their way
in order to help us.
Thank you for caring about us
and thank you for such loving people.

Let's Pray for People

We pray for people who are puzzled;
who can't quite work out what it is
that you are saying to them.
Please send people to them
who can help them to understand,
and make us all willing
to help one another.

About Turn!

This is the story of how someone changed. His name was Saul, and he lived at the same time as Jesus, but the story begins just after Jesus had gone to heaven. Jesus' disciples were going round all the country saying that Jesus was alive, and he was really the special person God had been promising to send, and lots of people were believing it and were becoming Christians*. Saul wasn't at all happy with that! He was a Pharisee, and we know how much the Pharisees had hated Jesus when he was on earth. Of course, they thought they'd got rid of him when he was crucified, and now here were his friends going round saying all these things! It seemed as though Jesus was stronger now than he ever had been!

There was only one thing to do. The religious authorities decided to kill as many followers of Jesus as they could; that should put anyone off from joining, they thought. It started with a man called Stephen who made the religious people so angry that they started a riot and stoned him to death. Saul was watching that, and he thought it was a good idea. He didn't join in – that would have been too undignified for a Pharisee – but he looked after people's coats for them while they did it.

After that, Saul really got the taste for it. He was so convinced that his was the only right religion that he just couldn't wait to start frightening Christians. He got people to spy on their friends; he sent agents out to listen at keyholes; he even got some people to pretend to be friends of Jesus, so that they could get into the meetings and give long lists of names to him afterwards.

Before long, it simply wasn't safe to be a Christian at all, but the strange thing was that people still kept on joining up. They seemed to be so convinced that Jesus was God's Son that they were prepared to die if necessary.

* According to scripture, the term 'Christians' had not yet been coined, but it is used here for the sake of simplicity.

Saul couldn't understand it. How could they be so wrong, and yet so committed? Deep in his mind, where he was hardly aware of it himself, a tiny bit of doubt began to grow. So Saul did what people always do when that happens. He worked even harder, to try and pretend that the doubts weren't there. Very soon he became really vicious, and went rampaging around chasing Christians and getting them killed. He was on the council, so after he'd caught them he would vote for the death penalty as well. He even tried to bully people into saying things they wouldn't have said. He was terrible!

Then, one day, someone told him about a group of Christians at a town called Damascus. 'What!' he said. 'Surely it hasn't spread as far as that! We've got to stop it before it goes any further.' He makes it sound like a nasty disease, doesn't he? And in a way that's what he thought it was – and the people were the germs that had to be killed.

Saul asked for an appointment with the High Priest. 'This new religion has spread to Damascus,' he said. 'If we don't stop it, it will be all over the world.'

'It's very worrying, I agree,' said the High Priest. 'What will happen to people like us if this new religion takes over? We could end up just like ordinary people!' The High Priest shuddered at the very thought of being 'ordinary', and went on, 'What do you think we should do?'

'Give me a warrant with your seal on it,' said Saul, 'and I'll take a few heavies with me and deal with them.'

The High Priest signed the warrant, and Saul went and got his mob together. Then they set off for Damascus. 'We'll show them who's really in charge of things!' he thought.

Along the road they travelled, with Saul getting more and more excited all the time as he tried to quieten that dreadful little voice inside him by saying nasty things about Christians, and what he was going to do to them. Suddenly, a bright light flashed from the sky; a light so bright that it made the midday sun seem quite dim! Saul didn't know what it was, but he did the only thing he could think of: he hit the deck! He buried his face into the sleeve of his coat, but he just couldn't shut out that light! Then he heard a voice, and this time he couldn't drown it out or pretend that it wasn't there.

'Saul, Saul, why are you persecuting me? Why are you fighting so hard against that inner voice?'

'Saul was terrified. 'Who are you?' he asked, although he was afraid he probably knew the answer.

'Don't give me that, Saul!' the voice answered. 'Deep down, you know who I am – you've been trying not to listen to me for months. I'm Jesus. I'm the one you're being so nasty to – because when you hurt my friends you hurt me, too.'

It was no good; Saul finally had to listen, and to hear what he had never wanted to hear.

'What shall I do?' he asked.

'Get up and go to Damascus. But instead of hounding the Christians, you're going to become one of them. And you're to tell everyone about me.'

So Saul got up, but he couldn't see anything. 'Gosh,' he thought. 'Talk about a blinding light!' He had to be helped by his friends, who couldn't understand what was happening.

When they got to Damascus, Saul was met by a Christian called Ananias. 'I don't know what's going on,' said Ananias, 'but God seems to want me to meet you. I hope you're not going to kill me and my friends.'

Ananias wasn't the only one who was surprised. The religious leaders in Damascus had been waiting for Saul to get rid of the Christians for them. Imagine their amazement when they found he was one of them!

Based on Acts 9:1-22

Let's Chat

Have you ever refused to listen to somebody,
because you were afraid they might be right?

We're Sad

Loving God, we don't always want to hear
what you are trying to say.
So we find ways of blocking it out.
Please forgive us, and don't give up
until we have given in!

We're Glad

Thank you, God, for not giving up on Saul,
and for not giving up on us.
Thank you for being patient with us,
and for offering us so many chances.

Let's Pray for People

We pray for people who are ignored;
people with really important things to say,
but things which other people
don't want to hear.
Please encourage them,
and let them believe
that it's worth carrying on trying.

God Has No Favourites

Cornelius was an officer in the Roman army. Although he was very generous, and had a lot of Jewish friends, he was not allowed into their houses and they couldn't go into his. That was because of the laws they had to observe, which may seem rather strange to us now but they were important to the people of the time. They had been conquered by different empires so often in their history that if they had not been very strict about their religion it might have died out altogether.

Cornelius used to read the Bible and he understood what the rule was all about, but he did sometimes feel very sad that he couldn't be more involved with his friends.

One day, Cornelius had a visit from an angel who had been sent with a very special message from God. Now Cornelius was a tough soldier, and he didn't frighten easily – he'd faced dangers and terrors which would make you or me run for miles! But all of those things didn't seem very much compared with being visited by an angel. What on earth could the angel want? What had Cornelius done that was so terrible that God was going to punish him personally?

That's the sad thing about religion, you see. For some reason, it so often makes people feel guilty even when they don't need to. Cornelius had no reason to be afraid of God; in fact the angel was there for the very opposite reason.

'Don't worry,' said the angel. 'God's sent me to say how pleased he is with you.'

'Well, bless me!' said Cornelius.

'Give me time,' said the angel. 'I was just coming to that. You've got to get in touch with a man called Simon Peter, who's staying at Joppa for the time being. He's lodging near the sea front with a leather worker called Simon. Yes, I know it's confusing – just be glad you don't know as many different Simons as I do! Anyway, it's Simon *Peter* you actually want. Ask him to come over and see you.'

Cornelius called his servant. 'Antonio,' he said, 'I've got a job for you.'

'Oh, dear, sir!' exclaimed Antonio. 'You haven't got blood on your best tunic again, have you? I do wish you'd be more careful. Remember what I've told you: it's off the peg battledress for killing and mutilating, and made to measure tunic and kilt for ceremonial parades only.'

'No, don't worry, Antonio – it's not that,' said Cornelius with a smile. 'I want you to go and look for a leatherworker.'

'Look for a leatherworker, eh?' mused Antonio. 'Obviously a case of "hide and seek". Get it? "Hide" and seek – you see sir, "hide" is another name for leather – oh, never mind. Where is this leatherworker, then?'

'He's in Joppa,' explained Cornelius. 'He lives right by the sea front.'

'Oh, does he!' returned Antonio. 'So I suppose when he goes home he goes "back to front"! No? Back to front? A pun, you see, sir – when he goes back, he has to go "back" to the sea front – oh what's the use!'

'Quite!' said Cornelius. 'Now I want you to ask for a man called Peter.'

'That sounds okay,' said Antonio. 'I'll just knock on the door and say . . .'

'I think the sooner you leave the better, don't you?' Cornelius interrupted him, and Antonio left, muttering to himself.

'Not much to ask, is it?' he chuntered, as he went down the hall. 'Just to work for a master with a sense of humour, who knows his best uniform from his battle dress – that's all! Not a lot to ask!'

Meanwhile, in Joppa, Peter was on the flat roof of Simon's house praying. He was hungry, and just as he was wondering whether dinner was ready yet, he had an amazing vision. He saw a great big sailcloth coming down out of the sky, as though it was held by the four corners. When it got low enough, he peeped over the side of it and saw lots and lots of different animals.

'There you are, Peter,' said God. 'Eat one of those.'

'I can't do that!' exclaimed Peter. 'Those are dirty animals – you know I can only eat the food which our religion counts as clean.'

'It's what I say that matters,' said God, 'and if I say something's clean, who are you to disagree?'

Altogether, this happened three times, and Peter was sure it must mean something but he couldn't work it out. Then, while he was still wondering, he heard a knock at the door; and when his friend Simon opened it Peter heard a voice say, 'Hello, I'm Antonio. I've come to see Peter. Can I see him, or is Peter out? Tee hee hee! Get it? "Peter out"? Oh, please yourself!'

'Hey, Peter!' called Simon. 'There's a comedian here to see you.'

'Oh, no!' thought Peter. Then he had an idea. 'Tell him he can't come in,' he called to Simon. 'He's a foreigner and he's not ritually pure.'

'I heard that,' Antonio shouted back. 'I'm as pure as you are. Anyway, it was your God who told my boss to send for you, so don't you come all that purity malarkey with me.'

Then Peter remembered what God had said in his vision: 'If I say something's clean, who are you to disagree?'

'Trust me,' he thought. 'I was just the same when Jesus was around – always going and putting my foot in it.' Then he called out, 'I'll be right down.'

Well, to cut a long story short – and spare you any more of Antonio's horrible jokes – Peter let Antonio stay the night, and then went with him to where Cornelius lived. He told Cornelius all about Jesus: about how the powerful people had killed him and how he'd risen from the dead. Cornelius looked a bit embarrassed at that, but Peter told him not to worry. 'It's the future that matters,' he said. 'You can't change the past, but you can help transform the future. That's what resurrection's about'

So Cornelius was baptised, and became a follower of Jesus, and Antonio did too.

'I've learnt a lot today,' said Peter. 'God really doesn't have any favourites – he loves everybody just as much.'

'That's wonderful,' said Cornelius, looking relieved. 'Does that mean he'll fix things so that I don't have to put up with Antonio telling me those dreadful jokes?'

'No,' said Peter. 'I'm afraid not.'

Based on Acts 10

Let's Chat

Do we ever behave as though
God loves us more than other people?

We're Sad

We're sorry, God, for wanting
to be your favourites.
Help us to remember that you love
everyone just as much.

We're Glad

Thank you, loving God,
for not having favourites.
Thank you for loving us all
even when we don't deserve it.
Thank you for always being here
and never leaving us on our own.

Let's Pray for People

Caring God,
there are people who think that
you don't love them.
They think that they're too sinful,
or the wrong race or colour.
This makes them very unhappy.
Please help us to show them
that you love them just as much
as you love other people.

THE ANGEL, THE APOSTLE AND THE GREAT ESCAPE

King Herod Agrippa was a rather unpleasant character who seemed to come from a long line of similar nasties. His great grandfather, Herod the Great, had tried to kill the baby Jesus, and Mary and Joseph had run away to Egypt to escape from him; then his father had been part of the plot to have Jesus crucified and now this Herod was following in Grandad's footsteps. He was terribly unpopular, and so he did what politicians nearly always do when they're unpopular – he looked for easy ways of making people like him.

Ever since the disciples had started telling people that Jesus had risen from the dead and gone to heaven, the powerful people had been spreading lies about them to make people hate them. So the Christians were almost as unpopular as Herod was. That gave Herod an idea. He had James, who had been one of the really close friends of Jesus, arrested and put in prison. That made Herod a little less unpopular, so he thought he'd go a bit further and he cut James's head off. He was right. The mob liked that very much indeed. 'This is a jolly good idea,' Herod thought to himself. 'I'm getting rid of Christians and making myself more popular both at the same time.' So he had Peter arrested, too. He put him in chains and then used sixteen guards working in four shifts to keep watch on him. He must have thought that Peter was really important to waste all that time and money on keeping him prisoner! And even then it didn't do any good.

One night, Peter was sleeping, chained up between two guards with the others keeping watch outside, and Herod was planning to put him on trial next day. It wouldn't be a *real* trial of course, just a pretend one. Herod could frighten or bribe a few people into telling lies and make sure a lot of people heard them, and then he could chop Peter's head off, too, and make himself really popular. What's that? You ask why he did all this? Well, it's very simple really, and very silly. The more power people have, the more they want and they'll do anything to avoid losing it. So, like his Dad and his Grandad before him, Herod thought it was quite all right to kill a few people if that helped him keep his power. Anyway, back to Peter.

Peter was asleep, chained and guarded, when he felt a tap on his shoulder. At first he thought it was the guards – they often used to keep people awake as a kind of torture – but it wasn't. Peter found that the cell was full of light, and there was an angel standing beside him. Well, he *thought* it was an angel – or was it?

'Hi there, Peter baby!' said the angel. 'Hey, what are you waiting for? Come with me – and look lively now. I haven't got all night.'

Peter thought this must be a dream. Well, wouldn't you? 'You don't talk like an angel,' he said.

'Takes all kinds to make a heaven, baby!' said the angel. 'Now are you coming? I've left a party that's out of this world to come and get you out, so show a leg. Put your coat on, though, 'cos Baby, it's cold outside. Now walk this way, son.' With that, the angel led the way, jigging and dancing and snapping his fingers as though he could hear music.

Now Peter was *sure* he was dreaming. 'If I could walk *that* way,' he thought, 'I'd be in show business.' Still, he thought, he might as well enjoy the dream. His chains had fallen off and were lying in a heap on the floor, between the sleeping guards. So he put his coat on and followed the angel out of the prison, past the guards who looked straight through them without seeing, and into the city. The angel was setting a cracking pace, and every so often, he would look round and say, 'C'm on, Peter baby – get with that crazy beat!'

Peter was really hoping that the dream wouldn't end too soon when the angel said, 'That's it, buddy boy. Got to get back. Wow-eeeee what a party!' And with that, he was gone, leaving Peter standing in the middle of the road on his own.

'It's not a dream,' Peter thought. 'It's true. God sent an angel to help me. Well, I think it was an angel . . . Yes, of course, Jesus always uses the last people you'd expect. It *was* an angel!'

The night was cold, just as the angel had said, and so Peter made his way to the house where Mary lived – no, not that Mary, there were Marys everywhere in those days. This Mary lived with her son, John Mark. Peter knocked on the door, and one of the maids, called Rhoda, came to see who it was.

'Ello! 'Oo is it?' she called through the door.

'It's me. Peter.'

'Go on!' answered Rhoda. 'You're 'avin' me on – Peter's in prison, Peter is.'

'Oh, come on, Rhoda – it's cold out here!' said Peter.

Then Rhoda recognised Peter's voice. 'Ooh it is!' she shouted. 'It's 'im! 'Ere, missis – you'll never guess 'oo's outside!' And she went running back into the living room, leaving Peter still standing outside in the cold. 'Oh, do be quiet, Rhoda,' said Mary. 'That's a very bad joke.'

'No, honest, it's 'im,' said Rhoda 'I allus know Peter's voice, 'cos 'e talks funny.'

Meanwhile, Peter was getting impatient and knocked more loudly on the door. 'Hey!' he called out. 'It's me you silly girl – open the door.'

Well, you should have seen Mary's face when she came to the door and found it really was Peter. Mind you, that was nothing compared with Herod's face when he found out that Peter was gone. He was furious! 'I don't believe it!' he screamed. 'Four of you, armed to the teeth, to guard one lousy prisoner who's chained and locked in a cell, and you can't even do that.'

'We're very sorry, Your Majesty,' said the chief guard. 'We just don't know what happened to him.'

'"Don't know"? "Don't know"?' screeched Herod. 'It's your perishing job to know. More to the point, it's your job not to let it happen. Now what am I going to do? I promised the people an execution – a nice juicy beheading. Well, someone's got to lose their noddle, and since you can't use yours you won't miss them will you? That's it! Call the executioner! Off with their heads!'

That's what power can do to people, you see. They get everything out of proportion, and start behaving irrationally. And in the end it didn't do Herod any good: all the power in the world wouldn't stop him from dying a horrible death.

It makes you think, doesn't it: there must be a better way of doing things.

Based on Acts 12:1-18

Let's Chat

Life's not very fair is it?
We all know how it feels to be blamed or punished
when we haven't done anything wrong.

We're Sad

Please forgive us, God,
if we've been unfair to people;
if we've blamed someone for something
without being sure it was their fault,
or let them take the blame
for something we have done.

We're Glad

Thank you, God, for caring,
and for setting people free.
Thank you for loving us, even when
we're not very loving to others.

Let's Pray for People

Lots of people need to be set free:
from prisons, but also from fear,
or from the unkindness of others.
We all need to be freed from our own prejudice,
or from being addicted to money or power.
Please God, send your angel
and set us all free!

Index of Bible References